# FINANCIAL RATIOS
# AND
# THE PREDICTION OF CORPORATE FAILURE

## About the Author

**DR. R.A. YADAV** is a senior Faculty Member in Northern India Banks Staff Training College, New Delhi. He topped Panjab University, Chandigarh in M. Com and subsequently obtained a Ph.D from University of Delhi. He has taught at Shri Ram College of Commerce, University, of Delhi before joining NIBSTC. He has published a number of research papers in reputed journals and is the author of a book 'Management and Monitoring of Industrial Sickness' which has won the DMA-ESCORTS Book Award-1986. The Institute of Chartered Accountants of India has announced the award of Best Article Prize 1986 to Dr. R.A. Yadav for the article on 'Working Capital Management - A Parametric Approach' Contribu by him to their Journal.

# FINANCIAL RATIOS AND THE PREDICTION OF CORPORATE FAILURE

RAM AVTAR YADAV

CONCEPT PUBLISHING COMPANY PVT. LTD.
NEW DELHI-110059

**ISBN: 978-81-7022-051-0**

First Edition 1986

*Published and Printed by*

Concept
Since 1974

**Concept Publishing Company Pvt. Ltd.**
A/15-16, Commercial Block, Mohan Garden,
New Delhi-110059 (India)
*T*: 91-11-41101460
*E*: publishing@conceptpub.com, *W*: www.conceptpub.com

*Dedicated*
*To*
*The Loving Memory*
*of My Teacher*
*(Late) Prof. S.S. Srivastava*

# Acknowledgements

It gives me a great pleasure to express my deep gratitude to my esteemed supervisors Professor R.S. Nigam, Head, Department of Commerce and Professor S.S. Srivastava, Faculty of Management Studies, University of Delhi, for providing me all the help and guidance for conducting this research work and in writing the thesis.

I wish to thank Professor L.S. Porwal, Department of Commerce, and Professor B.S. Yadav, Head, Department of Mathematics, University of Delhi, for initiating the problem and giving me the guidance during the initial stages of the research work. Professor Yadav has given me all the help I needed in the mathematical formulation of the problem.

I also thank Dr. L.C. Gupta, Dean, Research, Management Development Institute, New Delhi and Shri P.C. Jain, Lecturer, Shri Ram College of Commerce, for many fruitful discussions I have had during the course of my research work.

I am grateful to the Department of Company Affairs, Government of India, for providing the essential data for my project, the Computer Centre, University of Delhi, for great help in computation work and the staff of the Ratan Tata Library, Delhi School of Economics, for their cooperation.

I am thankful to the University Grants Commission for providing the financial assistance and to the authorities of Shri Ram College of Commerce, for giving me leave and other facilities while I was working on the project.

I am also thankfull to the Indian Council for Social Science Research for rendering the financial assistance for the publication of the work.

I thank Shri Thakur Dass for typing the manuscript.

Finally, credit is also due to my wife, Shyama, who has shared the strain of the thesis work with patience.

RAM AVTAR YADAV

# Contents

# Abbreviations

BSE = Bombay Stock Exchange
B/S = Balance Sheet
C = Cash
CA = Current Assets
CD = Current Debt
CF = Cash Flow from Operations
Co. = Company
DA = Defensive Assets
Dep. = Depreciation
DJSC = Directory of Joint Stock Companies
EBIT = Earning Before Interest and Taxes
FA = Fixed Assets
GR = Group
ICICI = Industrial Credit and Investment Corporation of India Limited
IFCI = Industrial Finance Corporation of India Limited
IRCI = Industrial Reconstruction Corporation of India Limited
Inv. = Inventory
Int. = Interest
LTD = Long Term Debt
NA = Not Available
NI = Net Income
NOP = Net Operating Profit
NS = Net Sales
NW = Net Worth
NWC = Net Working Capital

QA = Quick Assets

RBI = Reserve Bank of India

SIC = Standard Industrial Classification

TD = Total Debt

TOE = Total Operating Expenditures

TTA = Total Tangible Assets

# List of Tables

CHAPTER I

# Introduction

Throughout the past few decades, the accent in management literature and in research has been upon the achievement of success. The subject of company failure had received virtually little attention from writers, academics and management specialists. But in 1970, Penn Central, North America's sixth largest company collapsed—followed ten months later by Rolls-Royce. This caused a stir and a number of books and articles appeared on sickness. For decades now, the accepted criterion by which a company has been judged is how fast it has grown or how rapidly it has increased its market share. The concern about the failure of a company is also as much a part of a manager's task as the achievement of its success. It has been so in the past, it is more so now and will be more important in the future, for the penalties of failure are becoming more severe.

The failure of a business firm is an event which has always brought mental pain to entrepreneurs, managers and to their families. The society is also affected by business failure, as unemployment goes up, availability of goods and services decreases and the cost goes up. The shareholders lose their savings, creditors lose their cash and future business. The customer is deprived of the product. Therefore, a model which predicts the potential business failure at the earliest would serve to minimise, if not eliminate, such losses by providing ample warning in advance to all thosec oncerned. This need has been a sufficient motivation for me to chooset he prediction of corporate failure as an interesting and challenging area for investigation.

## 1.0 The Dimensions of Business Failure

The phenomenon of industrial sickness, both in large and small scale industry, has become alarming in recent years. Over Rs. 3200 crores are locked up in over 92500 sick units. These include both, small and large companies. This has been causing considerable concern to the government and the credit institutions. Whatever may be the reasons for such sickness, the common effects of such sickness are locking up of financial resources, wastage of capital assets, loss of production and employment.

The data availability position regarding business failure is itself far from satisfactory. There are no comprehensive reviews of sick industries published by the Government except occasional statements and announcements of Government take over of sick units. No doubt, the Reserve Bank of India [1] does collect some data on the subject, but that it does from a limited point of view—that of monetary involvement of banks in these units. These data do not indicate the actual or the likely loss of employment and output arising out of the sickness of the industrial units. The industry-wise break up of sick large and medium industrial units are summarised in Table 1-1.

Table 1-1 clearly points out that there were 325 large and medium scale industrial units at the end of June 1978, each of which had availed the bank credit of rupees one crore and above and which had been classified by the RBI as sick. The amount of bank credit locked up in and outstanding against them at the end of June 1978 was Rs. 956.08 crores. By the end of June 1979, the number of such sick industrial units had gone upto 345 and the amount of bank credit outstanding against these units had increased to Rs. 1101.72 crores. At the end of June 1983, Rs. 1913.10 crores of bank money was locked up in 463 sick industrial units which had further gone upto Rs. 2339 crores of bank money locked up in 544 sick industrial units by the end of December 1984.

In addition to the sick large and medium scale units, the number of sick small scale units had gone up from 16805 at the end of June 1979 to 92015 at the end of December 1984 and the outstanding bank credit had increased from Rs. 181.71

TABLE 1-1. **Number of Sick Industrial Units and Credit Outstanding: Industry-wise**

*(Amount in Rs. Crores)*

| Industry | June 1978 | | June 1979 | | June 1980 | | June 1981 | | June 1982 | | End-June 1983 | |
|---|---|---|---|---|---|---|---|---|---|---|---|---|
| | No. of Units | Credit Outstanding | No. of Units | Credit Outstanding | No. of Units | Credit Outstanding | No. of Units | Credit Outstanding | No. of Units | Credit Outstanding | No. of Units | Credit Outstanding |
| I. *Large and Medium Scale* | | | | | | | | | | | | |
| i) Engineering and Electricals } ii) Iron and Steel | 112 | 286.18 | 115 | 337.25 | 88 | 304.25 | 92 | 319.61 | 91 | 351.75 | 101 | 365.74 |
| ii) Iron and Steel | | | | | 42 | 82.36 | 47 | 105.89 | 40 | 142.31 | 38 | 142.45 |
| iii) Cotton Textiles | 78 | 263.65 | 84 | 287.71 | 89 | 349.56 | 94 | 406.48 | 114 | 520.24 | 119 | 579.83 |
| iv) Chemicals | 21 | 117.95 | 23 | 135.04 | 22 | 146.16 | 26 | 186.12 | 25 | 182.62 | 27 | 209.24 |
| v) Sugar | 31 | 79.48 | 35 | 100.95 | 48 | 77.97 | 48 | 117.00 | 45 | 148.23 | 44 | 180.11 |
| vi) Jute Textiles | 31 | 76.58 | 33 | 89.75 | 35 | 86.81 | 35 | 92.26 | 37 | 110.28 | 37 | 120.53 |
| vii) Rubber | 05 | 25.17 | 07 | 34.07 | 09 | 42.50 | 12 | 64.95 | 15 | 100.41 | 16 | 108.33 |
| viii) Cement | 04 | 13.69 | 04 | 13.21 | 03 | 11.83 | 03 | 13.20 | 03 | 12.08 | 03 | 09.23 |
| ix) Others | 43 | 93.38 | 44 | 103.74 | 53 | 131.26 | 65 | 147.78 | 69 | 160.48 | 78 | 197.64 |
| Total (I) | 325 | 956.08 | 345 | 1101.72 | 389 | 1232.70 | 422 | 1453.29 | 439 | 1728.40 | 463 | 1913.10 |
| II Small Scale | — | — | 16805 | 181.71 | 22325 | 292.80 | 22360 | 321.82 | 26973 | 393.67 | 64388 | 626.52 |
| Total (I+II) | 325 | 956.08 | 17150 | 1283 43 | 22714 | 1535.50 | 22782 | 1775.11 | 27412 | 2122.07 | 64851 | 2539.62 |

crores at the end of June 1979 to Rs. 879 crores at the end of December 1984.

Thus, taking the large and medium scale sector and the small scale sector together, it can be seen that the total number of sick industrial units in the economy rose from 17150 at the end of June 1979 to 92559 at the end of December 1984. The total amount of bank credit outstanding against sick units rose from Rs. 1283.43 crores at the end of June 1979 to Rs. 3218 crores at the end of December 1984.

The industry-wise break-up of sick large and medium scale units shows that units belonging to five industry groups—engineering, cotton, textiles, chemicals, sugar and jute textiles—account for the major share of bank credit locked up in such sick units. Of the total credit locked up in sick large and medium units, those belonging to these five industry groups accounted for 86.1 per cent at the end of June 1978, 86.3 per cent at the end of June 1979 and 84.21 per cent at the end of June 1982. Even within these five industry groups, units belonging to engineering and cotton textile groups accounted for more than 50 per cent of the total credit outstanding against all sick large and medium scale industrial units. The incidence of sickness is found more in the case of cotton textile industrial units. In the case of engineering and electricals, iron and steel and sugar industries, there was a reduction in the number of sick units, but the amount of credit outstanding increased by Rs. 32.14 crores, Rs. 36.42 crores and Rs. 31.23 crores respectively.

In Indian industrial scene, serious concern is generally echoed on the progressive increase in sickness in industry and the large resources being blocked in sick enterprises. However, a comprehensive study involving a forewarning system against corporate sickness is still lacking. A forewarning system is, thus, needed to detect potential business failure as early as possible so that timely action can be initiated to intervene. The intervention may involve change in management of the firm, grant of additional funds or funding by other organisations jointly to stem further sickness. Time and effort need be spent on diagnosing the causes of sickness and on deciding the kind of remedial action required in a particular case only after the forewarning system has identified a particular case as a potential sick unit. This need of evolving a forewarning system in this unexplored area has provided the impetus for conducting the present study in Indian context.

## 1.1 The Concept of Failure

Failure/sickness in industries has been viewed in several ways. Walter [2] and Donaldson [3,4] has termed it as technical insolvency when a firm is unable to meet its maturing obligations. Others restrict the term to the so-called real insolvency case where the total value of the firm's assets is smaller than its liabilities. Sometimes business failure is interpreted in the strict legal sense of bankruptcy or liquidation when the firm ceases its operations [5].

*According to ICICI*—'Sick Industry' is one whose financial viability is threatened by adverse factors present and continuing. The adverse factors might relate to management, market, fiscal burden, labour relations or any other. When the impact of these factors reaches a point when a company begins to incur cash losses leading to erosion of its funds, there is a threat to its financial viability. A sick unit is defined by the Reserve Bank of India [6] as 'a unit may be considered sick, if it has incurred cash losses for one year and in the judgement of the bank, it is likely to continue to incur cash losses for the current year as well as the following year and which has an imbalance in its financial structure such as current ratio of less than 1 : 1 and worsening debt equity ratio.' This definition seeks to emphasize operational performance and financial position which are inter-related to each other. Keeping the above in view, there can be at least three different view points in defining sickness:

(a) At the Government level in India, Corporate sickness gets recognised generally only when a unit is on the brink of closure or closes its doors, throwing a large number of people out of employment.
(b) At the lending institutions level, the problem gets recognised when non-payment of instalments due on money lent starts and continues for two or three intervals i.e. recovery of money lent becomes uncertain.
(c) From the Shareholders' point of view, an enterprise is

considered sick if it fails to pay reasonable dividends and the future also looks bleak and the share values tumble down.

A review of three different view-points defining sickness brings to bear that the third view is nearer the economic sense of the term 'failure' and related to the earnings potential of the enterprise and the second view is nearer the business sense of the term 'failure' and is related to the liquidity position of the enterprise.

Non-payment of dividends will almost invariably precede the default on debt obligations, and the default on the latter will ordinarily precede the cessation of operations. Hence, these different view points may be said to represent different stages of sickness. At what stage should sickness be recognised? How seriously sick must an enterprise become before it is labelled 'Sick'? Definitive answers to these questions are not possible, specially because the tendency towards sickness is not necessarily an irreversible process. It is rarely possible to say when exactly a particular unit fell ill. Therefore, a more specific definition of failure/sickness is needed. Our method of analysis should be capable of ascertaining the characteristic differences between the failed/sick and non-failed/non-sick companies. Keeping this practical objective in view, it was decided that the sample should include the known sick and non-sick companies, as the case may be, on reliable evidence. Only by a comparison of such known cases we shall be able to identify those characteristics which have the greatest forewarning potentials. Hence, failure/sickness is represented for the purpose of this analysis by entry into creditors' voluntary liquidation, compulsory winding up by the order of the court under the provisions of the companies act 1956 as amended from time to time, and the Government take over explicitly for reasons of sickness (as in the case of textile companies coming under the National Textile Corporation). This meaning has been adopted also because of the fact that it is difficult to prove or determine corporate failure/sickness in economic and business sense of the term except with the detailed case study of individual companies. In any case, such a discovery is only conceptual, whereas in the case of our definition of failure, it is a fact and the life of the company is annuled by legal action without doubt or ambiguity.

## 1.2 Failure is an Organic Process

Sickness in an industry is an 'organic process in the life history of a unit. A healthy unit may grow sick temporarily and may recover or vice-versa. Factors that cause sickness could be internal or external. The external factors usually affect all the industrial units in the same group while the internal factors may affect a particular unit only and not the whole industry. In such cases, the sickness has an origin followed by several stages of sickness. The sickness process is illustrated in Figure 1-1. Initially a healthy unit may show good cash profit and may have positive values of net working capital and net worth. As it tends towards sickness, the first (cash profit) may become negative although the unit may continue to pay its instalments to the term lending institutions. As sickness grows more and more through other stages, two or more financial parameters may become negative. The negative values do signal sickness. It is these initial stages that require careful monitoring. For such a purpose, a fore-warning system which signals the probable failure of industrial concerns before any loss is inflicted upon the concerned parties would prove to be a great boon. It would provide a warning to all the concerned parties to reconsider their situation and take prompt and appropriate action.

It is a well established fact that earlier the trouble is detected, more easily and economically it may be countered. Early detection of failure possibly may enable the management to take timely action to avert the crisis of such an occurrence. If there exists a forewarning system which helps in predicting corporate failure, the concentration can be focussed on those concerns which are trudging towards failure. The Chairman of the Industrial Finance Corporation of India (IFCI) mentioned on 33rd Annual General Meeting about the importance of an effective monitoring system:

'One is well aware of the sickness in industry. While it is not possible to avoid sickness in the industry entirely, it has come to be clearly recognised that i) this process can be

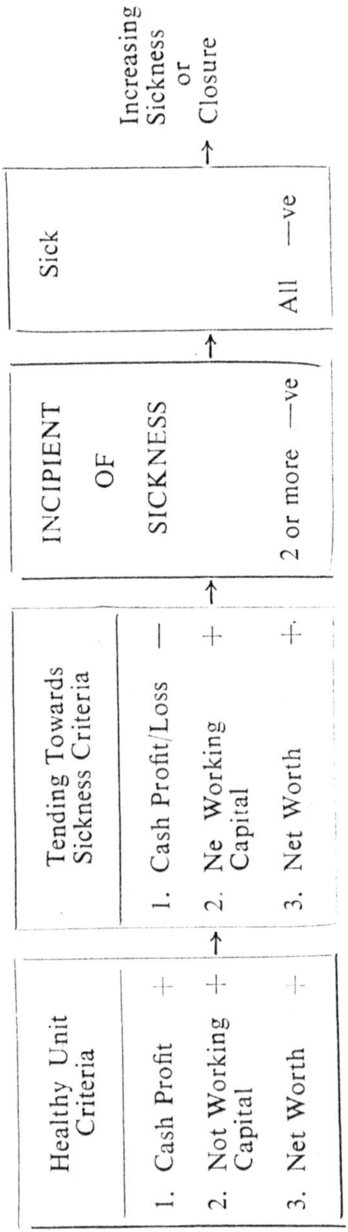


FIG. 1-1. *The Failure/Sickness Process*

considerably controlled with effective monitoring, and timely steps to ensure prevention of sickness, and ii) by rehabilitation of some of the units which have become sick, but which are potentially viable. This can be feasible only when some monitoring system is in force [7].'

Companies do not go burst 'overnight' as many people think. The process of failure can take years and thus the seeds of failure may be discernible very early in the story of a company's rise and decline. The forewarning system would help in reducing, if not completely eliminating, the irreparable loss to the interested parties caused by corporate collapse. The importance of such a forewarning system can be described in the words of Lev [8] more clearly:

'An early warning signal of probable failure will enable both management and investors to take preventive measures; operating policy changes, reorganisation of financial structure, and even voluntary liquidation will usually shorten the length of time losses incurred and thereby improve both private and social resources allocation.'

An early warning system against corporate sickness can be designed by using profit and balance sheet data available in company annual reports. The potential of using financial measures as outward signals for locating trouble spots arises from the fact that there is a fairly close inter-connection between financial performance and managerial effectiveness. If this were not so all forms of accounting control and reporting would be useless.

Financial statements are multifunctional, catering to the needs of several users, both from within and outside the economic unit viz., managers, creditors, investors, Government, employees etc. On the basis of the information gained from these financial statements, these varied users reach the decisions pertaining to their own areas of interests. Economic messages that the various users draw from these financial statements get facilitated when the individual variables are transformed into financial ratios. A 'Financial Ratio' is a quotient of two numbers, where both numbers consist of financial statement items. The usage of financial ratios is justified by the fact that the selection of pertinent material from a plethora of published information is more useful than wide and indiscriminate reading. Financial ratios serve this purpose by reducing the size of data disclosed in financial statements to the precise information. Laurent [9] in this context opines:

'In principle, the justification for employing financial ratio analysis to investigate a company's financial state is highly defensible. There are certain normative relationships existing between different financial components of a company as displayed in the balance sheet and revenue and appropriation account. The extent to which a company does or does not conform to these norms for the activities (industry) that it is engaged in, is indicative of something favourable or unfavourable, depending upon relationship being examined.'

If the actual relationship exhibits a significant departure from the normative relationship it acts as a precursor of some event in the future. The prediction of future event is of great interest to the varied users of financial statements since predicting is a necessary and prior condition for decision-making. The predictive capability of financial ratios has assumed high importance in the past few years and it is now used as criterion for judging the usefulness of ratios [10]. The predictive capability as a criterion for judging the usefulness of financial ratios is generally justified by the fact that it circumvents the enormity of task required for a complete specification of decision settings.

## 1.3 Objectives and Scope of the Study

Despite the voluminous literature which has been published on financial ratios, the principles of using these ratios for analysis have lacked scientific approach. The manner in which financial ratios are presently being applied to appraise corporate health is not very reliable and accurate. There is considerable vagueness and misunderstanding about which ratios are really significant and what values are really critical. The analysis about the importance of particular ratios is based more on subjective feeling, convention and belief rather than on clear empirical evidence. The validity of the conventionally prescribed rules of thumb is open to serious doubt in the absence of empirical verification and in the light of actual experience. Keeping the above in view, an attempt has been made in this study to show the way towards a more scientific approach in financial ratio analysis in predicting the corporate health and its chances of survival or failure. To delineate it further, the aim of the study is two-fold:

(1) To assess the quality of financial ratios as an analytical technique to evaluate the performance of business enterprises. For this purpose, the ability of financial ratios to predict corporate failure relative to random prediction is taken as an illustrative case.
(2) To verify the widely held beliefs in accounting literature regarding the comparative utility of various financial ratios.

This study is concerned with the problem of developing a forewarning system against corporate failure/sickness. An enquiry into the causes of failure/sickness has not been attempted.

### 1.4 Data Used for Analysis

The study is based upon the financial statements prepared under currently accepted reporting standards and examines the predictive ability of 36 financial ratios. The financial data for sample companies have been collected directly from company annual reports and the various issues of Bombay Stock Exchange Directory. The reference period is 1966-1980 (both years included). The companies used in the study are stratified over many industrial classes and limited to industrial concerns in the private corporate sector. The firms from the banking, investment and other non-industrial sector are not covered in the study. The initial sample includes 78 companies of which 39 are failed and 39 are non-failed. The matching of firms was done in terms of industry, size as indicated by paid up capital and capital employed, fiscal year and age. The financial data for a period of six years prior to the date of failure were collected. However, not all of these companies could be covered for each year because of non-availability of some annual reports for some years. Thus the number of companies in the initial sample varies slightly from year to year. For prediction purposes, a series of samples from homogeneous and non-homogeneous group of companies have been chosen which constitute the validation samples.

Though an attempt has been made thoroughly in the face of practical limitations of data and we feel a considerable sense of confidence in the conclusions drawn from the study, yet it is necessary to utter a warning here. The forewarning system designed in this study is based wholly on published financial statements of companies and as such, has its limitations. Financial ratios cannot be expected to do better than the financial statements, the basic source from which these are derived.

## 1.5 **Organisation of the Study**

The present chapter has dealt with the general introduction to the subject of financial ratios and corporate failure. The dimensions of business failure, the concept of failure, the process of failure, objectives and scope of the study have been explained in this chapter. Chapter II analytically reviews the empirical work in India and abroad in the area of evolving financial ratios for predicting corporate failure/bankruptcy. Chapter III outlines the research design used for the present study. The method of analysis and sampling procedure are fully explained in this chapter.

Chapter IV forms the core of the study and deals with the task of empirically testing a wide variety of financial ratios on univariate as well as multivariate basis. This part of the study is devoted to the presentation and interpretations of the empirical findings arrived at by applying statistical tests for the prediction of corporate failure. In Chapter V, the predictive accuracy of the model in both homogeneous and non-homogeneous groups of industry has been discussed. In the last Chapter VI, the concluding observations, applications of the model and directions for further research are discussed.

CHAPTER II

# Survey of Earlier Work

## 2.0 Introduction

The aim of this chapter is to review briefly and critically the empirical work done in the area of evolving financial ratios for predicting corporate failure/bankruptcy. Empirical work on financial ratios with a view to evolve a basis for forewarning/prediction of corporate failure is scanty, however, it is necessary to review critically the attempts made in this direction. Broadly the attempts made in this direction fall under two categories:

1. Those that essentially contain a list of the signs and symptoms that failing companies have exhibited; and
2. Those using financial ratios as detector or predictor of corporate failure.

Ross and Kami [11], Smith [12], Barmash [13] and others [14—18] have listed the signs and symptoms which become evident when companies start failing. However, the use of financial ratios as predictors of corporate failure can be viewed under three heads:

2.1 Univariate Empirical Work
2.2 Multivariate Models
2.3 Evaluation and Formulation of Hypotheses.

## 2.1 Univariate Empirical Work

*Paul J. Fitz Patrick*

Paul J. Fitz Patrick [19] conducted a study in 1932 to examine whether there was a significant difference in the trend of ratios for failed and non-failed firms at least three years prior to failure. He selected 19 companies randomly which had failed during the period of 1920-1929 and chose a matching sample of 19 successful companies using financial soundness, asset size, sales volume, product line and fiscal year as matching criteria. Each pair of firms was examined for three years prior to the date of failure. His objectives were to examine whether or not the ratios of successful companies were satisfactory when the ratios of failed concerns were unfavourable and whether the majority of the ratios of successful companies were favourable or unfavourable, and to what extent. He examined nineteen pairs of failed and non-failed firms using a number of financial ratios and evaluated to determine whether they met a certain minimum level and to identify the trends or tendencies they exhibited. The ratios of both the groups were compared with the minimum level and found that successful firms surpassed the minimum level in most of the cases, while, on the other hand, the ratios of failed firms were below the minimum level in majority of the cases. Also, the ratios were examined for any trends and found that the ratios of the failed firms deteriorated as the year of failure approached. He concluded that all the ratios of failed firms were persistently different from the non-failed firms at least three years prior to failure. It was observed that the net worth to debt and net profits to net worth were the best indicators of failure among the ratios used. Fitz Patrick concluded, "... that the ratios are important tools in ascertaining significant relationships of business fact. These relationships are worthwhile indicators, not absolute indicators of impending financial difficulties (19, p. 731].

*Winakor, Arthur and Smith, Raymond, F.*

Winakor and Smith [20] examined 183 firms which failed between 1923 and 1931 for ten years prior to the year of failure. The prior ten years trends of the means of twenty-one ratios of failed firms were analysed. A modified mean ratio was computed from the inner half of their data i.e.

$$(Q_3 - Q_1)/\tfrac{1}{2}\ N.$$

Failure was defined as either entering receivership, bond

default or material readjustment of rights or equities of owners and creditors. Twenty-one ratios for each of the firms were computed and examined after the financial statements had been standardised. The mean ratios of the middle half of all the firms were used to compare individual changes for the whole group. Other groupings, which included four different industries and two size groups (less than three million dollars and greater than 20 million dollars) were also used. For these, the arithmetic mean of the groups was compared with the accepted minimum levels. It was concluded that the ratios of the failed firms were frequently below the mean value used for comparison and showed deterioration as the date of failure drew near and also pointed out that the ratios of net working capital to total assets (NWC/TA) was the most accurate and steady indicator of failure, with its decline beginning ten years before the occurrence of failure. It was concluded that for the 183 companies studied, the ratios of working capital to total assets was a far more steady and accurate, as well as an earlier indication of unfavourable trends in financial health. Unlike the Fitz Patrick study, there was no corresponding group of successful firms in this study.

*J.R. Ramser and L.O. Foster*

Ramser and Foster [21] analysed eleven types of financial ratios for 173 firms whose securities were registered in the state of Illinois. It was found that firms which turned out to be less successful and those which failed tended to have ratios which were lower than the more successful firms. However, two turnover ratios—sales to net worth and sales to total assets, exhibited an opposite tendency.

*Evaluation of Three Studies*

These studies suffered some shortcomings. Fitz Patrick's sample was small and too selective to generalise the conclusions. In the study of Ramser and Foster, many of the differences were more apparent than real. Winakor and Smith study suffered the shortcoming of lacking a contrasting control group of successful firms.

However, in general the shortcomings of these three studies were outweighted by the essential importance of their contribution. They represented an extremely significant event in the development of ratio analysis because they were the first carefully developed attempts to utilise the scientific method for determining the utility of ratios for predicting the sickness of firms.

*Charles L. Merwin*

Merwin [22] using a sample of over 900 firms of continuing and discontinuing firms corroborated the ratio differences for as far back as six years before failure. This study of the relationship between financial ratios and business failure concentrated on small corporations (under $ 2,50,000 in total assets) which failed during the period 1926-36. Merwin analysed the prior six years trend of a large, unspecified number of ratios of continuing and discontinuing firms. Two methods of comparison were used. One was to determine a high-low range for each ratio, for every year, by using the surviving companies as indicators of what the highs and lows should be. The other method was to use an 'estimated normal' ratios reflecting the success of the surviving firms. The estimated normal ratios are estimates of what the discontinuing firms ratios would have been if they had maintained the same average ratios as the surviving firms.

Comparing industry mean ratios of disappearing firms against estimated normal ratios and the high-low range of ratios, it was found that the ratios of the discontinuing companies were consistently below the 'estimated normal' and out of line with the high-low range established by the surviving firms. A persistent decline from the 'estimated normal' was also found beginning with the sixth year prior to failure. It was concluded that three ratios were sensitive predictors of failure upto as early as four to five years prior to discontinuance. These three ratios were: (1) Net working capital to total assets, (2) the current ratio, and (3) Net worth to total debt. One of these, net working capital to total assets, was found to be the best 'single indicator of failure'. A test of statistical significance showed that the probability of getting the above results would be less than .01. With these results, Merwin concluded that the deviations of certain credit ratios from an empirically determined level has definite diagnostic value. In other words, if the ratio persists in moving in an adverse direction, that movement is portentous of business discontinuance. This does not mean that a company having this financial experience will inevitably discontinue operations. It does signify, however, that an unhealthy condition is developing which, unless corrected will result in business discontinuance. Merwin's study was the first really sophisticated analysis of ratio predictive power, and the findings of the study still appear to be credible. Thus, the usage of some ratios was indicated formally.

*Hickman, W.B.; Saulinier, R.J.; Moore, G.H.; Atkinson, T.K. and Saiden, M.H.*

Hickman [23] found that the times-interest-earned ratio and the net profits to sales ratio were useful predictors of the default experience of corporate bond issues during 1900-1943. Saulinier [24] found evidence from RFC lending experience during 1934-1951 that borrowing firms with poorer current ratios and net worth to debt ratios were more prone to loan default. Moore and Atkinson [25] found that the ability to obtain credit was correlated with several ratios. Saiden [26] reported that certain financial ratios (e.g. Net working capital to total assets) were inversely correlated with an index of trade credit difficulties. This series of studies used ratios as variables for examining and describing economic activity, thus further widening the empirical base of ratio analysis. In these studies, additional evaluations of predictive power of ratios were made. It was concluded that financial ratios provided an insight into the firm's capability to obtain credit and repatriate the credit obtained.

*Beaver's Model*

Beaver [27] was among the first to focus on the ability of ratios to predict failure. Failure was defined as the inability of a firm to pay its financial obligations as they mature. Operationally, Beaver defined corporate failure rather broadly. The firm was considered failed firm when any of the following events had occurred: bankruptcy, bond default, an over-drawn bank account or non-payment of preferred stock. A univariate prediction model of corporate failure was developed and tested on observations of 79 failed and 79 non-failed firms over the period 1954-1964. The sample consisted of 79 failed firms and 79 non-failed firms, selected by paired sample technique. He collected data of 79 firms which failed between 1954 and 1964 and matched them by industry, asset size and fiscal year to similar data of 79 firms which had not failed. The objective of such a sample design (paired sample) was to mitigate any effect that asset size or type of industry might have on the possibility of failure. The financial data of the failed corporations were grouped by year, prior to failure, for five years, and were matched with the financial statements of the non-failed firms. Thirty (30) financial ratios [Appendix A] over a period of five years prior to failure (the period chosen for study) were computed for each of the 79 failed and 79 non-failed firms. Beaver had three type of analysis in order to establish the predictive power of financial ratios: (1) a comparison of mean values, (2) a dichotomous classification test; and (3) an analysis of likelihood ratios. First, Beaver compared the mean values of the ratios which he called a profile analysis. A comparison of the mean ratios for the failed provided substantial evidence that the financial ratios of failed firms showed deterioration and were worse than that of non-failed firms as early as five years prior to failure.

A comparison of the mean ratios for the failed and non-failed firms corroborated the findings of earlier studies [19,20,22]. The evidence showed that the difference in the mean values is in the predicted direction for each ratio in all five years before failure. Failed firms not only have lower cash flow than non-failed firms, but also have a smaller reservoir of liquid assets. Although the failed firms have less capacity to meet obligations, they tend to incur more debt than do the non-failed firms. The trend line of the non-failed firms has a zero slope, and the deviations from the trend line are small. Yet the deterioration in the means of the failed firms is very pronounced over the five years period. The difference in mean is evident for at least five years before failure, with the difference increasing as the year of failure approach. The evidence overwhelmingly suggests that there is difference in the ratio of failed and non-failed firms.

The second type of analysis (i.e. Dichotomous classification test) was made to test the existence and extent of predictive power of ra'ios. The dichotomous classification test predicts the failure status of a firm, based solely upon a knowledge of the financial ratio. The technique used is as follows:

The firms are randomly divided into two sub-samples. For a given ratio, the data of the first sub-samples are arrayed in ascending order. The array is inspected to find an optimal cut off ratio, a cut off point that minimizes the percentage of incorrect predictions. If a firm's ratio is below the cut off ratio, the firm is classified as failed and vice-versa. The optimal cut off point for the first sub-sample was used to predict the failure status of firms in the second sub-sample. Similarly, an optimal cut off point was derived for the second sub-sample and was used to predict the failure status of the firms in the first sub-sample.

Comparison of the actual status of the sampled firms with the predicted one resulted in the percentage of firms misclassified. Lower the error of prediction, the greater the predictive power of ratio. The ratio with the smallest percentage error was considered the best predictor. Dichotomous classification test indicated that the most successful predictor was the cash flow to total debt ratio. In the first year before failure the error was only 13 per cent, while in the fifth year, the percentage of error was 22 per cent. By using cash flow to total debt ratio as the best predictor of failure, Beaver computed the classification error rates (presented in Table 2-1) over a period of five years prior to the failure.

The comparison of random prediction (P=50%) with the prediction through financial ratios provides evidence that the failure status of the firm can be predicted correctly to a much greater extent than could be expected from the random. It was concluded that ratios were useful in predicting failure for at least five years before failure, but the predictive power of all ratios was not equal and ratios did not correctly predict failed and non-failed firms with the same degree of success. The

TABLE 2-1. **Predictive Accuracy of Beaver's Cash Flow to Total Debt**

| Year Before Failure | % of Correct Classification | % of Error |
|---|---|---|
| 1 | 87 | 13 |
| 2 | 79 | 21 |
| 3 | 77 | 23 |
| 4 | 76 | 24 |
| 5 | 78 | 22 |

classification error was more in case of failed firms than non-failed firms.

However, Beaver was not satisfied with these results, because the choice was treated as dichotomous and therefore, the magnitude of the difference between the ratios and the cut off point was not considered, while predicting the probability of failure. To overcome these problems, Beaver undertook an analysis of likelihood ratios. The likelihood ratio analysis indicates the extent to which a decision maker's assessments of the probability of failure are altered by looking at the financial ratios. In order to assess the likehood ratios from the financial ratios, histograms were prepared and inspected. The conclusion of the analysis of likèlihood ratios supported that the ratios were useful indicator of failure of the firm at least five years prior to failure.

In his second study 1968 [28] by using the same data he computed in the study of 1966, Beaver applied the concept of liquidity. The main purpose of this study was to test whether liquid or non-liquid asset measures were better predictors of solvency. It was concluded after examining the data by using his methods of analysis (i.e. Profile analysis, dichotomous classification test and analysis of likelihood ratios) that the non-liquid asset measures were far better predictors of corporate failure as contrary to a prior belief in the liquid asset measures.

Being aware of the limitations in using only accounting

data, Beaver extended his study to a comparison of the predictive power of financial ratios with that of stock market prices [29]. In this study he examined the impact of market prices in the prediction of corporate failure. Using the original sample of data, Beaver found that stock market prices indeed predicted failure sooner than individual financial ratios. Beaver concluded that, 'the findings of the cross-section and time series analyses were uniformly consistent with respect to two major contentions:

(1) Investors recognize and adjust to the new solvency positions of failing firms;
(2) The price changes of the common stocks act as if investors rely upon ratios as a basis for their assessments, and impound the ratio information into the market prices.

However Beaver cautioned against taking these results at face value, because of the limited scope of his study.

Beaver's work was one of the most complete study of the relationship between financial ratios and business failure, however, it had its limitations and was criticised on the ground of being a univariate approach.

## 2.2. Multivariate Models

### *M. Tamari*

Tamari's [30] was the first multivariate study in which weighted composite of several ratios were used to indicate the possibility of failure. He introduced a few financial ratios in the model generally accepted in the literature and practice as indicators of financial soundness. These selected ratios were given certain weights according to their importance in the eyes of financial analysts, economists and creditmen. He attached weights to the ratios which were combined in a subjective manner.

Profit trend and equity capital and reserves to total liabilities ratios were given maximum weights relatively showing that these ratios were considered to be best indicator of failure. To test his *index of risk*, he compared the value of his induction for failed companies in the year prior to failure against the value of index for all industrial companies between 1956-1960. He observed that 75 per cent of the failed firms had less than 35 points and 50 per cent had less than 25 points. Tamari pointed out that ratios were only indicators and that low values were not proof of future bankruptcy. His general conclusion was that firms with less than 30 points are more likely to go bankrupt than those with over 60 points. Similarly there is a little likelihood that firms with a high index will drop to a low category. These conclusions were confirmed by the empirical verification that 50 per cent of the firms securing less than 30 points failed while only three per cent of firms with more than 30 points failed. Only one per cent of the firms securing less than 30 points rose to over 60 points and none of the firms coming in the category of over 60 points fell into the lower category (below 30 points).

The main criticism levelled against Tamari's study was that both the ratios and relative weights used in the index were somewhat arbitrarily chosen. The choice of ratios and relative weights were based on writer's own experience, without any conceptual or empirical support. The resulting indices were, therefore, of questionable generality.

### *Altman's Discriminant Model*

Altman [31] developed a model for the prediction of corporate bankruptcy using a sample of 33 bankrupt and 33 non-bankrupt matching firms over the period of 1946-1965. Multiple Discriminant Analysis (MDA), the most advanced statistical technique used so far was applied to discriminate the bankrupt firms from non-bankrupt firms on the basis of financial ratios. He first developed a predictive model using MDA and then examined the predictive ability of the model. His discriminant model was an attempt to overcome the shortcomings of single ratio analysis incorporated in other studies. His analytical technique (MDA) was directly concerned with the problem of distinguishing between bankrupt and non-bankrupt firms prior to actual bankruptcy.

Multiple discriminant analysis is a statistical technique used to classify an observation into one of several a priori groupings dependent upon the observation's individual characteristics. It is used primarily to classify and/or make predictions in problems where the dependent variable appears in qualitative form e.g. male or female; bankrupt or non-bankrupt. After the groups are established, data are collected for the objects in the groups; MDA then attempts to derive a linear combination of these characteristics which best discriminates between the groups.

Altman used a paired sample consisting of thirty three failed and thirty three non-failed manufacturing firms, where industry and size were used as the matching criteria. Twenty two (22) financial ratios were considered in various combinations as predictors of failure. The ratios which were included and the weights given were determined by the significance of the contribution they made to the predictive ability of the model. The final set of ratios was determined by F-tests and computer runs analysing the possible alternatives. The following combination (i.e. discriminant function) of five ratios did the best overall job in discriminating between the failed firms and non-failed firms:

$$Z = .012X_1 + .014X_2 + .033X_3 + .006X_4 + .999X_5$$

where Z=overall index

$$X_1 = \frac{\text{Working Capital}}{\text{Total Assets}} \quad \text{(a liquidity measure)}$$

$$X_2 = \frac{\text{Retained Earnings}}{\text{Total Assets}} \quad \text{(a measure for reinvested earnings)}$$

$$X_3 = \frac{\text{Earning before Interest and Taxes}}{\text{Total Assets}} \quad \text{(a profitability measure)}$$

$$X_4 = \frac{\text{Market Value of Equity}}{\text{Book Value of Total Debt}} \quad \text{(a measure for the firms financial structure or leverage)}$$

$$X_5 = \frac{\text{Sales}}{\text{Total Assets}} \quad \text{(a measure for the sales generating ability of the firm's assets)}$$

A cut-off point for the Z score was determined in such a way as to minimise the overlap between bankrupt and non-bankrupt groups. He concluded that the Z score of 2.675 was the best cut-off point which maintained minimum misclassification. Using discriminant function, he conducted several tests to ascertain the accuracy of the model. The Z value was computed for each company and based on this score and on the cut off point determined earlier, the particular company was classified as bankrupt or non-bankrupt. Table 2-2 given as under shows the classification accuracy of the model.

TABLE 2-2. **Classification Accuracy for Predicting Future Bankruptcy (Altman's Model)**

| Year Before Failure | % of Correct Classification | % of Error |
|---|---|---|
| 1 | 95 | 05 |
| 2 | 72 | 28 |
| 3 | 48 | 52 |
| 4 | 29 | 71 |
| 5 | 36 | 64 |

From the table it appears that the discriminant function correctly classified 95 per cent of the total sample one year prior to failure, but the predictive accuracy declined to 72 per cent when data of two years prior to bankruptcy were used. When the data of three, four and five years prior to failure were used, the predictive accuracy of the model reduced to 48, 29 and 36 per cent respectively and the predictive power of the model became unreliable. Altman further tested his model on a secondary sample taken irrespective of its size, and industry and formed the predictive power to be similar to that reported above, 96 per cent correct classification. He applied the scaled vector to determine the relative contribution of each variable to the total discriminating power of the function and interaction between them. Earning before interest and taxes to total assets ratio contributed the most in the group discriminant function.

In one [32] of the few other studies [32-36] explaining corporate failure with new variables [Appendix B], Altman used MDA once again with both linear and quadratic structures. In this study he concluded that the newer Zeta model predicted better than his earlier model. The classification accuracy of bankrupt firms for five years before failure was 69.8 per cent using Zeta analysis and 36 per cent using 1968 model.

The lead given by Altman in applying the MDA technique to predict corporate failure was followed by several researchers though differ from Altman's in respect of the variables included in the discriminant function.

*Deakin's Model*

Motivated by the contribution of Beaver and Altman in constructing the prediction model in predicting the corporate failure, Deakin [37] developed an alternative model for predicting failure. He conducted a study to predict corporate failure taking a sample of thirty-two failed firms and a matching sample of thirty-two non-failed firms. The failed firms' sample included those firms which experienced failure between 1964-1970. Like Beaver and Altman, each of the failed firms was matched with a non-failed firm on the basis of type of industry, year of financial data provided and asset size in order to mitigate the impact of industry, size and year of information on failure. Deakin's original model included 14 ratios and his revised model included only 5 ratios which could best predict corporate failure in each of the five year's prior to failure. He defined failed firms as those which experienced bankruptcy, insolvency or were otherwise liquidated for the benefit of creditors.

First, Deakin adopted a method of analysis similar to the Beaver's study by applying the dichotomous classification test, he ascertained the percentage error of each ratio [Appendix C]. To get additional insight into the operations of failing companies, he made the comparison of mean values of ratios and used Spearman's rank-order correlation coefficient to indicate the order of predictive power of ratios. He observed higher correlation of relative predictive ability of various ratios. The rank-order correlation coefficients were found to be significant in four of the five years. The correlation coefficient in the third year before failure was relatively very low. To find out why the coefficient was low, a comparison of mean values of the ratios was made, which indicated that the failed firms tended to expand rapidly in the third and fourth year prior to failure. It was observed from the analysis of Capital Structure that the expansion was financed by increased debt and preferred stock rather than common stock or retained earnings.

Funds raised were invested in fixed assets (plant and equipment) rather than in liquid assets. These firms were unable to generate the sales and thus net income to support a heavier debt and, therefore, they lost their assets rather rapidly after the third year prior to failure.

In the second test, Deakin used discriminant analysis using the same sample of data and 14 financial ratios as input to the discriminant analysis programme. The output from the programme consisted of a set of discriminant weights which indicated that linear combination of variables maximising the difference between the groups as well as the scaled vector which indicated the relative contribution of each variable. The misclassification error rates, as predicted by the model, were 3 per cent, 4.5 per cent and 4 per cent for the first, second and third years respectively. The classification error rates increased rapidly to 21 per cent and 17 per cent in the fourth and fifth year respectively. The results of testing the model on independent sample drawn at random consisting of 11 failed and 23 non-failed firms were 22 per cent, 6 per cent, 12 per cent, 23 per cent and 15 per cent error rates respectively for the five years prior to failure. It was concluded that the discriminant analysis can be used to predict business failure using ratios as prediction of failure three years in advance with a fairly high degree of accuracy [Appendix D].

### *Pifer's Model*

Meyer and Pifer [38] developed a linear regression model for the prediction of bank failures. He selected a sample of 78 banks consisting 39 failed banks which experienced failure during the period 1948-1965 and 39 solvent matching banks. The paired sample was taken on the basis of location (same city), size, age and regulatory requirements. Thirty two financial ratios were used as independent variables in the various regression models tested. Financial ratios were computed for the period of six years prior to failure. A step-wise regression programme, forward selection and backward reduction at each step was used. A classification test used by Meyer and Pifer correctly predicted 80 per cent of the initial sample banks and 72 per cent of the banks in the hold-out sample with a lead time of one or two years before failure. When the lead time was three or more years, the model failed to discriminate between failed and non-failed banks. Thus, they concluded that financial ratios were to be used alongwith other factors such as local economic conditions, general economic conditions, quality of management, integrity of employees to make a better prediction of bank failures.

### *Marc Blum's Failing Company Model*

The Failing Company Model (FCM) was developed by Marc Blum [39] to assess the probability of business failures. The operational definition of failure used in this study was an inability to pay debts as they become due, entrance into bankruptcy proceedings or an explicit agreement with creditors to reduce debts. Discriminant analysis was applied to a paired sample of 115 failed and 115 non-failed firms to evaluate the predictive accuracy of the model.

In order to match failing firms with similar non-failing firms, sampling was based on four criteria, utilised in the following order—industry, sales, employees and fiscal year. These criteria were selected to eliminate the impact of industry, size and the year of information on the probability of business failure. Data drawn from balance sheets, income statements and stock market prices for a consecutive period of at least three years were collected for 115 companies which failed during the years 1954-1968 and matching 115 non-failed companies.

Blum developed a cash-flow framework for variables selection. He treated the business firm as a reservoir of financial resources and described its probability of failure in terms of expected flow of these resources. According to this cash flow framework, other things being equal, the probability of failure is more likely:

1. the smaller the reservoir,
2. the smaller the inflow of resources from operations in both the short-run and long run,
3. the larger the claims on resources by creditors,
4. the greater the outflow of resources required by operations of the business,
5. the more highly variables are earnings required and claims against resources required by the operations of the business,
6. the more 'failure prone' the industry locations of a firm's business activities are expccted to be.

The failing company model included 12 variables [Appendix E] and was constructed with reference to the three common denominators—Liquidity, Profitability and Variability—underlying the cash flow framework.

The accuracy of the failing company model in distinguishing failing firms from non-failing firms was tested by using discriminant analysis for computing an index and a cut off point on the index. Companies getting index score above cut off point were classified as non-failed companies and all companies with scores below the critical point were predicted to fail. The model predicted the corporate failure with an accuracy of approximately 94 per cent, when failure occurred within one year from the date of prediction, 80 per cent for failure two years into the future and 70 per cent for failure three, four and five years distant. The model is to be considered more reliable on account of two reasons as advanced by Blum—the choice of each of its variable is justified on the basis of financial theory (i.e. cash flow framework), and the aforementioned results are the product of a rigorous validation procedure.

An experiment was also conducted to test the predictive accuracy of a non-ratio model. Five of the nine ratios used in the FCM were broken down into their eight independent variables and were used with the four non-ratio variables to form a non-ratio model. When tested the non-ratio model, while not as accurate as the Failing Company Model in the first year before failure was found to be consistently more accurate thereafter.

A regularly updated version of the Failing Company Model, was not found to improve its predictive accuracy. The new measure 'going to the Market' indicated the stock market's inability to anticipate reliably the timing of failure.

Relative importance of the variables comprising the FCM could not be assessed definitely. Nevertheless, cash flow to total debt ratio, found to be the best predictor by Beaver's research, received generally high ranking. When compared with other studies of business failure, the FCM was found to be more reliable than reported multivariate models, but when compared with Beaver's results, it was found that the predictive accuracy of the model was similar to the results of univariate approach. This was surprising since the multivariate FCM included Beaver's best ratio and was expected to be more accurate than a univariate approach. The conclusion reinforces the need for further research.

One more observation was also made by Blum that inventory declined rapidly for failing companies, which shows that, in general, firms do not seem to fail for reasons of excess accumulations of inventory, at least as shown by annual financial reports. Total debt of failed firms increased more than those of non-failed firms rapidly. It indicated that debt was a usual way for failing firms to finance growth.

### *Richard Taffler and Howard Tisshaw's Work*

Taffler and Tisshaw [40] developed a 'Z model' for the prediction of company insolvency and the evaluation of corporate creditworthiness by banks, investment houses and credit controllers. To construct a solvency model, a statistical technique known as 'linear discriminant analysis was applied to a sample of 46 failed firms and 46 financially sound firms matched by size and industry. Eighty different ratios were calculated for each of the 92 companies. Failure was defined as the firm's entry into receivership, creditors' voluntary liquidation, compulsory winding up by order of the court or government action undertaken as an alternative. Extensive statistical analysis finally isolated that set of ratios which discriminated best between the two sets of firms and resulted in the following discriminant function:

$$Z = C_0 + C_1 R_1 + C_2 R_2 + C_3 R_3 + C_4 R_4$$

where Z = discriminant score

$C_0$ = a constant

$C_1 ... C_4$ = the ratio weights or coefficients

$R_1$ = Profit before tax/current liabilities

$R_2$ = Current assets/total liabilities

$R_3$ = Current liabilities/total assets

$R_4$ = No credit interval ratio
(e.g. CA-CL/Operating cost excluding dep.)

The four ratios, taken together, measure the risk profile of the firm which was summarised by the single number, its Z-score.

It was concluded that:

'Take profit before tax divided by current liabilities; current assets as a proportion of total liabilities; current liabilities as a proportion of total assets; take into account the 'no credit interval'; mix them in the right proportions and you can tell whether a company will go burst' [40, p. 50].

### *Ohlson's Logit Model*

Ohlson [41] developed a conditional logit model which pointed out that the fundamental estimation problem can be simply reduced to the following statement:

'Given that the firm belongs to some prespecified population, what is the probability that the firm fails within some prespecified time period'. The conditional logit model made no assumption regarding prior probabilities of bankruptcy and for the distribution of predictors.

He used a sample of 105 firms which experienced bankruptcy during the period 1970-1976 and 2058 non-bankrupt firms. Nine financial ratios [Appendix F] were computed and tested to form an opinion about the discriminatory power of fin ancial ratios. First, he made the use of profile analysis technique which explained that ratios deteriorate as one moves from two years prior to failure to one year prior to failure of firms. The standard deviations of the ratios were larger for bankrupt firms compared non-bankrupt firms, the differences were found to be significant at 5 per cent level. Three set of estimates were computed for the conditional logit model. The results indicated that the four factors derived from financial statements were statistically significant in assessing the probability of bankruptcy. They are: (1) size, (2) the financial structure as reflected by a measure of leverage (TLTA), (3) some performance measures (NITA) and/or (FUTL), (4) some measures (s) of current liquidity (WCTA or WCTA and CLCA jointly). Some other tests were also conducted taking some more measures of profit margin, and a ratio of assets with or no cash value divided by total assets and found these as significant variable for purposes of assessing solvency status of a firm.

*Dambolena's Work*

Dambolena and Khoury [42] constructed a model using stability and level of financial ratios as explanatory variables in the derivation of discriminant function. The basic purpose of this study was to test the effect of stability of financial ratios on prediction of corporate failure. 19 ratios were selected as predictor variables and their measures of stability were used for the purpose of prediction in this stability model. A sample of 46 firms was taken and four measures of stability were computed for each of the 19 ratios and for each of the 46 firms for the period of 1969-1975. The four measures of stability were:

1. the standard deviation of the ratios over three years period;
2. its standard deviation over four years period;
3. its standard error of estimate around a four linear trend; and
4. its coefficient of variation over four years period.

When empirically tested, the ratios with their standard

deviations and ratios alone provided almost the same results for one year prior to failure. However, the improvement was observed for three years before failure. When ratios alone were used, there was 70 per cent predictive accuracy of the model for five years before failure, but on the other hand, it increased to 83 per cent when the standard deviations (stability measures) were introduced. They concluded that the inclusion of stability of ratios in the analysis improved considerably the ability of the discriminant function to predict failure. The predictive accuracy of the model was 83 per cent on initial sample and 78 per cent on validation sample five years prior to failure, which indicates an improvement over the results of previous studies.

*R.A.I. Van Frederikslust's Work*

Frederikslust [43] made an attempt to predict business failure based on testable financial theory of corporate failure. He defined failure as a negative cash balance which was expressed in the following general form:

$$\begin{aligned} CB_t = {} & CB_{t-1} + S_t - (AR_t - AR_{t-1}) + OI_t \\ & - GS_t - GA_t - (BI_t - BI_{t-1}) \\ & + (SD_t - SD_{t-1}) + ALD_t. \end{aligned}$$

where

$CB_t$ = cash balance at the end of period t

$S_t$ = sales in period t

$AR_t$ = accounts receivable in period t (including prepaid expenses)

$OI_t$ = other income (including liquidation of assets) in period t

$GS_t$ = 'necessary cost of goods sold in period t'

$GA_t$ = 'necessary general administrative (including interest) and sales expenses in period t'

$BI_t$ = business inventories at the end of period t

$SD_t$ = short term debt (including repayment of long term debt) at the end of period t

$ALD_t$ = the additional long term debt obtained in period t.

A firm will fail at a certain moment t when its cash balance is smaller than zero. Thus failure was defined as $CB_t < 0$.

On the basis of financial theory he identified the following observable failure prediction variables: liquidity, profitability, solvability, variability of liquidity and variability of profitability overtime, industry variables and general economic variables.

A sample of 20 Dutch firms (excluding plantations) which failed during the period 1954-1974 and a matching set of solvent firms was taken from the Amsterdam Stock Exchange. The matching sample was selected from the same industry with approximately the same assets size and was measured over the same chronological period as the failed firm.

For each of the firms, the values of the prediction variables—liquidity and profitability were calculated for each of the five prediction years. This was done on the basis of uniformized financial statements. These variables were used to discriminate between two groups—failed firms and non-failed firms. To discriminate between failed and non-failed firms, a separate equation was computed by using multiple regression computer programmes for every prediction year. The prediction equations for each year of prediction (5 years) are of the form:

$$Y_1 = .5293 + .4488x_1 + .2863x_2$$

$$Y_2 = .4885 + .4859x_1 + .3789x_2$$

$$Y_3 = .4086 + .5760x_1 + 1.2731x_2$$

$$Y_4 = .4215 + .3095x_1 + 1.0977x_2$$

$$Y_5 = .3808 + .2602x_1 + .6986x_2$$

where $Y_1 \ldots Y_5$ = the regression score of the firm for one year to five year prior to failure.

$X_1$ = the liquidity ratio of the firm

$X_2$ = the profitability ratio of the firm.

The above equations statistically discriminated between the two groups and Lachenbruch's [44-45] method was used to determine the predictive accuracy of the model [Appendix G]. The two-variables using data of one year before bankruptcy correctly classified 92.5 per cent of the total sample which reduced to 82.5, 77.5, 72.5 and 70 per cent respectively when data of two, three, four and five year prior to bankruptcy were used. The predictive accuracy of the model was better for the non-failed than for the failed group. The classification error rates were more or less similar when the model was applied on secondary sample. The model was then extended by adding additional variables—the growth rate, the prediction error in the prediction year, and the coefficient of variation for both liquidity and profitability, but the predictive ability of the model was not significantly improved [Appendix H].

However, Fredrickslust tried to develop a bankruptcy prediction model based on a testable financial th-ory of corporate failure, but could achieve it partially. As he defined failure as a negative cash balance, but he changed this definition to bankruptcy or liquidation when the empirical work was undertaken. Since many firms had negative cash balances from time to time and were not bankrupt. He should have indicated how bankruptcy and a negative cash balance are identical.

Apart from the studies summarised above, there are few empirical studies which used alternative approaches to the problem of predicting failure of firms [46-51].

Now the few studies, though scanty, conducted in India for the prediction of sickness or failure status of a firm are summarised as under:

### *L.C. Gupta's Work*

Gupta [52-54] has made an attempt to examine, both statistically and in terms of logic, a wide variety of ratios and determine the best set of ratios. These are best not only for the specific purpose of identifying potential sick firms but also for the more general purpose of ordering firms according to financial health. A simple non-parametric test for measuring the relative differentiating power of the various financial ratios was used. The test was based on taking a sample of sick and non-sick companies, arraying them by the magnitude of each ratio to be tested, selecting a cut off point which will divide the array into two classes with a minimum possible number of misclassifications, and then computing the percentage classification error.

The sample included 41 textile companies of which 21 were non-sick and 20 were sick. The list of sick companies was prepared from four sources:

i) Sick Cotton textile companies coming under NTC;
ii) Companies assisted by the I.R.C.I.;
iii) Companies listed as sick by the ICICI in its portfolio; and
iv) Other companies taken over by Central Government explicitly for reasons of sickness.

The non-textile sample included 39 companies, of which 21 were non-sick and 18 were sick. The matching was done on the basis of product or products manufactured, age and size measured in terms of paid-up capital, assets and sales. In all, 56 financial ratios were selected for testing and computed for each of the company in sample for each year of 13 year period i.e. 1962-1974.

The empirical tests clearly showed that among profitability ratios, earning before depreciation interest and taxes to sales (EBDIT/Sales) and operating cash flows to sales (OCF/Sales) are the best ratios in predicting future bankruptcies. These two ratios had the least classification error among all profitability ratios for the textile companies sample during 1962-1964. Their classification error rates were about 11-13 per cent in 1962 and only 8 per cent in 1964 and still less thereafter.

A little inferior to the two ratios cited above were following three:

(a) EBDIT/TA+Acc. Dep,
(b) OCF/TA+Acc. Dep., and
(c) EBDIT/(Interest+.25 Debt.).

In order to minimise the classification error rates, he recommended a combination of the following four profitability ratios:

i) EBDIT/Sales (net of excise)
ii) OCF/Sales (net of excise)

iii) EBDIT/(Total Assets+Accumulated Dep.)
iv) OCF/(Total Assets+Accumulated Dep.).

The ratios relating to net worth were found to be worst predictor of bankruptcy among profitability ratios.

Among balance sheet ratios, the empirical tests showed that the solvency ratios were more reliable indicators of strength than any liquidity ratios. The following two were the best balance sheet ratios:

i) Net Worth/Total Debt.
ii) All outside Liabilities/Tangible Assets or Net Worth/Tangible Assets.

It was observed that companies with an inadequate equity base had little 'reserve strength' to weather adversities and are, therefore, sickness-prone. Another important observation of his study was that all liquidity ratios proved to be very poor predictors which contradict the great importance traditionally attached to liquidity analysis in appraising corporate health. The current ratio, for example, showed an average classification error almost three times more than profitability ratios in case of textile companies.

*Kaveri's Model*

Kaveri [55] attempted to predict the borrower's health by using financial ratios as predictors variables. To predict the event, a sample of 524 small units comprising of good, regular and sick units was taken. The units were defined as good, regular and sick on the basis of irregularity in the account. This classification was suitable for commercial banks for assessing credit requirements, follow-up action and review of the account.

In all 22 financial ratios were computed for identifying the health of small scale industries and were classified into five categories namely working capital, turnover, assets usage, profitability and financial stability. The ratios were reduced to a set of five variables by using statistical techniques such as F-test, T-test, scaled vector and multiple discriminant analysis.

The five ratios found to be statistically significant and acceptable to the bankers were the current ratio, stock/cost of goods sold, current assets/net sales, net profit before taxes/ total capital employed and net worth/total outside liabilities.

The multiple discriminant analysis technique was applied to develop a model consisting of five ratios to assign units in the sample to one of the groups viz., good, irregular and sick. The model was tested on initial sample and hold out sample for a period upto seven years before the event. The model correctly classified 76 per cent of units in the initial sample and 69 per cent units in the hold out sample for one year before the event [Appendix I]. It was found that the accuracy of the model was reduced as the lead time before the event increased. It is logically true as argued by Kaveri that as the lead period before the event increases, the ratios of a firm become less and less clear and, therefore, the accuracy of the model would be reduced accordingly. The accuracy of the model in the hold out sample was lower than the accuracy of the model in the initial sample.

### *S.S. Srivastava's Work*

A combination of operational, technical and financial parameters was used to discriminate between the sick and healthy units [56]. He developed a linear discriminant function comprising seven ratio parameters—five financial, one technical and one operational. These ratios were net worth/total assets, net block/net worth, net profit/total assets, total liabilities/net worth, current assets/current liabilities, capacity utilisation ratio and plant utilisation ratio. Initially a computer model was built up using three financial ratios and predictive accuracy of the function was computed.

The classification error rate was 15 per cent of this linear discriminant function which reduced to 10 per cent when only five financial ratios were applied. It further reduced to 5 per cent when first three ratios were combined with technical and operational ratio. The model was enlarged to include all the seven variables which resulted in 100 per cent predictive accuracy of the model at 1.0 per cent level of significance [Appendix J].

## 2.3 Evaluation and Formulation of Hypotheses

In most of the above mentioned studies on prediction of financial sickness or soundness of the firm, the researchers have explored a number of financial ratios as predictors of corporate failure and incorporated a large number of financial ratios in their predictive models. In brief, the purpose of these studies has been:

1. to investigate whether financial ratios are the significant variables to predict the survival or failure of the firms; and
2. to detect the ratio or a set of ratios taken together which are good predictors or indicators of such an event.

However, the evidence of these studies clearly indicates that with a few financial ratios, the survival or the failure of the firm can be predicted at least five years prior to the date of failure. Table 2-3 given below indicates the results of few

TABLE 2-3. **Percentage Classification Error Rates for Predicting Failure**

| Year Before Failure | Beaver's CF/TD | Altman's Discriminant Function | Edward Deakin's Model | Marc Blum's Failing Company Model |
|---|---|---|---|---|
| 1 | 13.0 | 05.0 | 03.0 | 07.0 |
| 2 | 21.0 | 28.0 | 04.5 | 20.0 |
| 3 | 23.0 | 52.0 | 04.5 | 30.0 |
| 4 | 24.0 | 71.0 | 21.0 | NA |
| 5 | 22.0 | 64.0 | 17.0 | NA |

selected studies which have pointed out that the failure of the firm can be predicted five years earlier. Observed evidence for five years prior to failure supports the view that financial ratios can be used in the prediction of failure.

Their conclusions, however, differ regarding the question of which ratio or set of ratios perform well as indicators of failures. This might be partly on account of the use of different research methodology used by the above mentioned researchers, for example, Beaver used univariate approach while multivariate approach was adopted by Altman. A major criticism levelled against most of these studies is that little consideration has been given to establish the relationship between financial ratios and corporate failure. Apart from this, on account of lack of consensus regarding the inclusion of ratios in the final profile as indicator or predictor of failure, the results of the above mentioned predictive models could not be generalised and, therefore, require further verification of their applicability. The researchers, however, have the merit of having demonstrated the power of financial ratios to predict financial problems of the company. It is also evident that relatively lesser number of ratios are sufficient to predict the chances of survival or failure of a company.

The studies conducted for predicting company failure are scanty in India [52, 55, 56-60]. Very little progress has been made in empirical testing of financial ratios with a view to showing which of them really reflect a company's state of health, its chances of survival or failure. Since no serious systematic attempt has been made in this direction, an attempt, therefore, is made in this study to show the way towards a more systematic and scientific financial ratio analysis for predicting the chances of survival or failure of a company.

Keeping in view the observations made in various studies conducted abroad and few in India, the following hypotheses are formulated for testing in the present study:

1. $H_0$=Financial ratios used univariately and/or multivariately cannot discriminate between the financial state of health of failed companies and non-failed companies.

   $H_1$=Financial ratios used univariately and/or multivariately can discriminate between the financial state of health of failed companies and non-failed companies.

2. $H_0$=Financial ratios used univariately and/or multivariately cannot predict the chances of survival or failure of a company or companies.

   $H_1$=Financial ratios used univariately and/or multivariately can predict the chances of survival or failure of a company or companies.

3. $H_0$=There is no relative difference in the predictive power of financial ratios in discriminating between failed companies and non-failed companies.

   $H_1$=There is relative difference in the predictive power of financial ratios in discriminating between failed companies and non-failed companies.

On empirical testing if $H_0$ holds true, the null hypotheses will be accepted. If $H_0$ is not valid, the null hypotheses will be rejected and it will be contended that a particular financial ratio or a set of financial ratios taken together possesses/possess the forewarning capacity to predict the chances of survival or failure of a company or companies and do possess relative predictive power in discriminating between failed companies and non-failed companies.

CHAPTER III

# Research Design

## 3.0 **Introduction**

The objective of this chapter is to present the design of research to be adopted for the study. The chapter lists the nature of information required, sources of data, sample, variables, and period selected for the study; and statistical techniques applied to test the formulated hypotheses.

The schematic presentation of the chapter is as follows:

3.1 Sample Selection and Data Collection: This section contains description of the nature of information sought for the study and the tapping of sources to collect such information. The period selected for the study and the rationale thereof has also been described in this section.

3.2 Development of the Model: This section contains the procedure adopted for the selection of variables for the study and the description of statistical techniques applied to test the hypotheses formulated.

3.3 Accuracy and Validity of the Model Developed.

## 3.1 **Sample Selection and Data Collection**

### 3.1.1 *Nature of Information*

At the outset, an attempt was made to identify the informations required and the sources to collect the same. The following informations were identified for the present study:

1. A set of failed companies and matching non-failed companies in the private manufacturing corporate sector;

2. Information in respect of the above identified companies:
   (a) Industry
   (b) Size
   (c) Age (i.e. date of establishment and failure)
   (d) Type of organisation.
3. Financial statements of companies one to six years prior to the event (i.e. failure).

### 3.1.2 *Selection of Failed Companies*

The selection of failed companies for which the financial data could be obtained was the most difficult task of data collection. After discussing the nature of problem with the representatives of several institutes (i.e. The Institute of Chartered Accountants of India; The Research and Statistics Division, Department of Company Affairs, Govt. of India, New Delhi; practising Chartered Accountants and Academicians) who might have access to such information, it was decided to take the primary list of failed companies from the Directory of Joint Stock Companies in India—a Yearly publication of the Research and Statistics Division, Department of Company Affairs, New Delhi and from the Company News and Notes—a monthly publication of The Department of Company Affairs, Govt. of India. Since the study is basically concentrated on the manufacturing public undertakings in the private corporate sector, the sample excludes the private limited companies and non-manufacturing companies (i.e. Public Utility Companies, Transport Companies, Trading Companies and Financial Institutions).

To begin with, those companies that had failed (i.e. reported to have gone into liquidation) during the period under study (1966 to 1980, both years included) were identified in the Directory of Joint Stock Companies in India and the Company News and Notes and compiled in a list. The compiled list of failed companies was condensed into a list that satisfied the following four conditions:

1. the company reported had gone into liquidation during the period under study (1966 to 1980, both years included);

2. the company is classified as manufacturing unit as per the Standard Industrial Classification (SIC) system of the Department of Company Affairs, Govt. of India;
3. the company is a public limited company; and
4. finally, the availability of financial data of the company for at least one year before failure.

Any failed company listed in the first tested by the above mentioned four criteria was included in the final list of initial sample of failed companies. The final list of failed companies contains 39 companies on which financial data could be obtained for first year before failure. The frequency distribution of the financial year of failure is presented in Table 3-1 given below:

TABLE 3-1. **The Frequency Distribution of Years of Failure**

| Year of Failure | No. of Failed Companies |
|---|---|
| 1966 | 2 |
| 1967 | 1 |
| 1968 | 0 |
| 1969 | 1 |
| 1970 | 0 |
| 1971 | 1 |
| 1972 | 6 |
| 1973 | 5 |
| 1974 | 3 |
| 1975 | 5 |
| 1976 | 7 |
| 1977 | 4 |
| 1978 | 2 |
| 1979 | 2 |
| 1980 | 0 |
| Total | 39 |

Next, the failed companies are classified according to industry and size as measured by paid-up capital and capital employed. Capital employed means the funds employed in the long run i.e. capital employed=share capital+reserves and surplus+long term loans. Each company is assigned a three digit code number, that the first digit denotes its group-1 (i.e. failed companies group) and next two digits denote its serial number in the group. The industrial composition and size classification of failed companies in the sample is shown below in Table 3-2.

TABLE 3-2(A). **Industrial Composition of Failed Companies in the Initial Sample**

| Co. Code Number | Industry | No. of Failed Companies |
|---|---|---|
| 101, 104, 110, 119. 123, 129, 132 | Cotton Textiles | 7 |
| 118 | Jute Textiles | 1 |
| 105, 116, 125 | Sugar | 3 |
| 102, 107, 124 | Food Products | 3 |
| 109, 113, 135 | Iron and Steel | 3 |
| 115, 138 | Electrical Equipment | 2 |
| 121, 127, 130, 131, 133, 139 | Machinery and Accesseries | 6 |
| 103, 111, 117, 120, 122 | Chemicals and Pharmaceuticals | 5 |
| 126 | Structural Clay Products | 1 |
| 106, 108, 114, 134, 136 | Glass Works | 5 |
| 112, 128, 137 | Paper and Paper Products | 3 |
| | Total | 39 |

The size as indicated by the capital employed of each company is taken from the most recent Balance Sheet of the company prior to the date of failure. The industry and size,

TABLE 3-2(B). **Size Pattern of Failed Companies in the Initial Sample**

| Range Capital Employed in Rs. (000) | No. of Failed Companies |
|---|---|
| 200—2500 | 15 |
| 2500—5000 | 3 |
| 5000—7500 | 2 |
| 7500—10000 | 8 |
| 10000—12500 | 3 |
| 12500—15000 | 4 |
| 15000—17500 | 1 |
| 17500—20000 | 1 |
| 20000—22500 | 2 |
| Total | 39 |

measured in terms of capital employed, composition of failed companies are heterogeneous. Table 3-2 (Part A and B) indicates that 39 failed companies operated in 11 different industries and the capital employed size range is 2 lakhs to Rs. 225 lakhs and the average capital employed size is approximately Rs. 71 lakhs.

### 3.1.3 *Selection of Non-Failed Companies*

Recognising the heterogeneity of failed companies sample, due to industry and size differences, a careful selection of non-failed companies was attempted on the basis of stratified sampling. The stratification of failed companies according to industry, capital employed size and fiscal year was taken as an essential prerequisite to the selection of non-failed companies. The companies were stratified by industry and size, with the capital employed size range restricted to between Rs. 2 lakhs to 250 lakhs. The mean capital employed size of the non-failed companies group (Rs. 80.48 lakhs approximately) is slightly greater than that of failed group, since the matching of exact size of the two groups was not feasible. The selection process of non-failed companies was based upon paired sample design i.e. for every failed company in our list of failed group, non-failed company of the same industry, of the same financial year and of almost the same size as indicated by paid up capital and capital employed in the financial statement one year prior to failure, was selected.

To match non-failed companies with failed companies and to reduce sampling biasness, sampling of non-failed companies was based upon three criteria, since the empirical works [61-64] have indicated that ratio differences exist because of the variables such as size, industry and fiscal period for which the ratios are calculated:

(1) Non-failed companies were chosen from the same industry as that of the failed company;
(2) of almost the same capital employed size as that of the failed company; capital employed and paid up capital were used as one of the matching criteria because they tend to be more stable over a period of time compared to other measures of size such as sales, net worth and output; and
(3) the data collected were of the same financial year as that of the failed company.

The names of non-failed companies were taken from the Directory of Joint Stock Companies in India (DJSC)—a yearly publication of the Department of Company Affairs, Govt. of India and the various issues of Bombay Stock Exchange (BSE) Directory and compiled in a list possessing two convenient features:

(a) the companies were grouped according to industry as per the Standard Industrial classification system of the Department of Company Affairs, Govt. of India; and
(b) within each industry group, the companies were ranked according to size as indicated by capital employed.

The following procedure was adopted to reduce the list of non-failed companies to the final list (i.e. 39 companies) of matching sample of non-failed companies:

(1) the industry number of a failed company was taken,
(2) that portion of the list of non-failed companies was opened where companies of that industry number were found;
(3) within that industry group, tentatively a company was selected whose size measured in terms of capital employed was closest to the size of the failed company;
(4) if the financial statement of the non-failed company for the same period as that of the failed company (i.e. preceding year before the failure) was available, it was selected as one of the non-failed company to be studied;
(5) if the company did not satisfy condition no. 4, the list of non-failed companies was reopened and tentatively the company next closest in size was selected;
(6) this procedure was repeated until a matching non-failed company was found; and
(7) this procedure was repeated for each of the failed companies in the sample.

The paired sample design was chosen to reduce and control over the impact of other factors—industry, size and fiscal year that otherwise might have blured the relationship between financial ratios and failure. The ratio literature indicates that industry factor must be incorporated in any complete ratio analysis [65]. It is stated in the ratio literature that the same numerical value of a ratio (e.g. current ratio of 2.0) may imply different probability of failure in different industries. The evidence offered on behalf of industry differences is the fact that the ratio distributions differ among industries [66].

Size measured by capital employed and paid up capital was the next important criteria for matching sample design. There are certain statistical reasons for believing that size alters the relationship between financial ratios and failure. It can be argued that smaller of the two companies will have more probability of failure, even if the financial ratios of the two companies are identical. Secondly, the rate of return to the company will become more stable as size increases. Empirical evidence indicates that the variability of rate of return does behave in this manner [67]. It indicates that the larger companies are less prone to failure even if the value of their financial ratios is the same as that of smaller companies. The financial ratios, therefore, of different asset size companies cannot be directly compared.

However, the use of matching sample design limits the scope of inferences in atleast one respect. It is possible that the industry and size may be excellent predictors of failure which is eliminated by the use of matching sample design. Thus, the findings will not provide any insight into the potential predictive power of industry and size when applied to the initial sample, though the model developed on the basis of initial sample has been applied on additional samples taken irrespective of industry and size in order to see the impact of these factors on failure.

An important issue was to determine the size, as indicated by capital employed, of the failed companies to be sampled. The big size companies were excluded from the sample since the incidence of failure in big-sized companies is rare, on the other hand, the absence of data negated the representation of too small companies. Therefore, to choose companies in initial sample of failed group in a restricted capital employed size range was not feasible, while random selection of non-failed companies irrespective of asset size seemed unwise.

Thus, the final list of the initial sample [Appendix K] contained 78 companies i.e. 39 failed companies and 39 non-failed companies.

### 3.1.4 *Collection of Data*

After defining the initial sample groups and selecting companies to be included in the final list for study, the next task was to collect the required data from the annual financial statements of both the failed and non-failed companies. The financial statements collected were the annual reports prepared under currently accepted reporting standards of Companies Act, 1956.

The data were collected primarily from two sources:

1. Various issues of Bombay Stock Exchange (BSE) Directory; and
2. Annual Reports of Companies (i.e. Balance Sheets and Profit and Loss Accounts) from the Library of the Company Law Board, Govt. of India.

A large proportion of financial data of failed companies for six years prior to failure were obtained from the Library of the Department of Company Law Board, Govt. of India. For some of the financial data of failed companies, various issues of Bombay Stock Exchange Directory were also consulted. A large proportion of annual reports of matching non-failed companies were taken from the various issues of Bombay Stock Exchange Directory.

The first year before failure is defined as that year included in the most recent financial statement prior to the date of company's failure. The second year before failure is the financial year preceding the first year. The years from third to six prior to failure are similarly defined. For example, a company failed in 1978 and the most recent financial statement was prepared on December 30, 1977, the first year before failure would include 1977 financial statement and the sixth year would include the financial data of 1972. The financial data of the matching non-failed companies were collected for the same financial years as those of their failed mates. The financial data of the non-failed companies were also stratified into year before failure, corresponding to the years that were assigned to their failed mates. For example, the financial statement of 1977 of a non-failed company to the matching failed company mentioned above would be assigned to the first year before failure and the statement of 1972 would be assigned to the sixth year before failure.

In the process of data collection, it was found that financial data were not available for each year before failure. The number, therefore, of companies in the sample decreases as the leadtime before failure increases. As availability of data, except the first year prior to failure, over a period of all six years was not the criteria to include a company in the initial sample. Table 3-3 given below indicates that the sample size is the largest in the first year before failure (i.e. 78 companies) and is the smallest in the sixth year before failure (i.e. 51 companies):

TABLE 3-3. **Number of Observations on which Financial Statement Data could be Obtained**

| Group | Year Before Failure | | | | | |
|---|---|---|---|---|---|---|
| | 1 | 2 | 3 | 4 | 5 | 6 |
| Failed Companies Group-1 | 39 | 39 | 37 | 35 | 29 | 26 |
| Non-Failed Companies Group-2 | 39 | 39 | 39 | 37 | 34 | 25 |
| Total | 78 | 78 | 76 | 72 | 63 | 51 |

For purposes of failure prediction, financial statement data were collected for the period of six years before the event (i.e. failure). The justification for the six years as a period for prediction of company failure is provided by the fact that previous studies indicated that financial ratios beyond five years prior to the failure have very limited predictive power. Most of the studies on bankruptcy prediction (discussed in Chapter II) provide evidence that financial ratios are not useful for prediction beyond five years prior to the bankruptcy. However, we have extended it upto six years to have the insight into the prediction of company failure prior to six years. Secondly, it is a sufficient time for testing the vibration in the profitability and liquidity reserve strength of a company to be considered. The period chosen for the study is 1966-1980. This fifteen year period is the most recent period for which the data, particularly of failed companies, were available.

## 3.2 Development of the Model

### 3.2.1 *Selection of Variables (i.e. Financial Ratios)*

The emphasis upon financial ratios as predictor variables does not imply that ratios are the only predictors of failure. The concern is not with predictors of failure, but rather with financial ratios as predictors of important event i.e. company failure. Further, the primary concern is not with ratios as a form of presenting financial statement data but rather with the underlying predictive ability of financial statements themselves. The ultimate motivation is to develop a model which can verify empirically the predictability of financial ratios. Financial ratios as predictor variables for the prediction of company failure are primarily selected on the basis of their ex-hypothetic capability to indicate the financial soundness or sickness of a company and on the basis of their proven performance in earlier studies (discussed in Chapter II).

The construction of a model designed to predict the company's chances of survival or failure involves few specific problems which were classified into two categories:

1. Choosing the variables i.e. financial ratios to be included in the model;
2. (a) Deciding upon the mathematical relationships among the variables; and
   (b) Assigning relative weights to the variables.

Three specific questions were raised to answer the above problems:

1. What criteria are to be used in order to choose the variables i.e. financial ratios for the study?
2. Which ratios must be combined together in a specific case i.e. prediction of chances of survival or failure of a company?
3. What weights must be attached to the ratios in a certain set of combination or combinations?

A list of 36 financial ratios were selected for the construction of a predictive model which were primarily conditioned by the objective of study and the availability of financial statement data which permitted the calculation of financial ratios.

The following guidelines were used to select the 36 ratios from the sets of all possible combinations and permutations of financial statement items:

1. The popularity in the literature i.e. the frequency of appearance of financial ratios in the literature [8, 65, 68-79];
2. The financial ratios performed well in one of the earlier studies (refer Chapter II]. However, there are certain ratios which performed well in predicting the chances of survival or failure of a company in recent empirical work, but were not included in this study on account of non-availability of relevant data e.g. Altman's market value of shares/Book Value of Debt; Gupta's EBDIT/TA+Acc. Dep.
3. The ratios defined within the framework of cash flow concept in which the company has been treated as a reservoir of financial resources and the probability of failure is described in terms of expected flows of these resources. Within the cash flow framework concept, other things being equal, the probability of failure of a company is smaller:
   (a) the larger the reservoir;
   (b) the larger the net liquid flow from operations (i.e. cash in flow);
   (c) the smaller the amount of debt held; and
   (d) the smaller the fund expenditures for operations.
4. The potential relevency of ratios for the study.

The presence of any one of the criteria was considered a sufficient condition for inclusion of a ratio in the study.

For every set of financial statement available, 36 financial ratios were computed for each of the year and classified under four groups depicting different aspects of company's operations. Financial ratios used for developing the failure-prediction model are as under:

I. *Profitability Ratios*

(*a*) *Cash Flow Ratios*

$V_1$. Cash Flow to Net Sales (CF/NS)
$V_2$. Cash Flow to Total Tangible Assets (CF/TTA)
$V_3$. Cash Flow to Net Worth (CF/NW)
$V_4$. Cash Flow to Total Debt. (CF/TD)

(*b*) *Income Ratios*

$V_5$. Net Income to Net Sales (NI/NS)
$V_6$. Net Income to Total Tangible Assets (NI/TTA)
$V_7$. Net Income to Net Worth (NI/NW)
$V_8$. Net Income to Total Debt (NI/TD)
$V_9$. Earning before Interest and Taxes to Total Tangible Assets (EBIT/TTA)
$V_{10}$. Earning before Interest and Taxes to Net Sales (EBIT/NS)
$V_{11}$. Net Operating Profit to Net Sales (NOP/NS)
$V_{12}$. Earning before Interest and Taxes to Interest (EBIT/Interest)
$V_{13}$. Net Income to Net Working Capital (NI/NWC)

II. *Solvency Ratios*

$V_{14}$. Total Tangible Assets to Current Debt. (TTA/CD)
$V_{15}$. Total Tangible Assets to Long Term Debt. (TTA/LTD)
$V_{16}$. Total Tangible Assets to Total Debt (TTA/TD)
$V_{17}$. Net Worth to Total Debt (NW/TD)
$V_{18}$. Net Worth to Long Term Debt (NW/LTD)

III. *Liquidity Ratios*

(a) *Liquid Assets to Total Tangible Assets Ratios*

$V_{19}$. Cash to Total Tangible Assets (C/TTA)
$V_{20}$. Quick Assets to Total Tangible Assets (QA/TTA)

$V_{21}$. Current Assets to Total Tangible Assets (CA/TTA)

$V_{22}$. Net Working Capital to Total Tangible Assets (NWC/TTA)

(*b*) *Liquid Assets to Current Debt Ratios*

$V_{23}$. Cash to Current Liabilities (C/CL)

$V_{24}$. Quick Assets to Current Liabilities (QA/CL)

$V_{25}$. Current Assets to Current Liabilities (CA/CL)

IV. *Turnover Ratios*

$V_{26}$. Net Sales to Debtors (NS/Debtors)

$V_{27}$. Net Sales to Inventory (NS/Inv.)

$V_{28}$. Net Sales to Quick Assets (NS/QA)

$V_{29}$. Net Sales to Current Assets (NS/CA)

$V_{30}$. Net Sales to Net Working Capital (NS/NWC)

$V_{31}$. Net Sales to Total Tangible Assets (NS/TTA)

$V_{32}$. Net Sales to Net Worth (NS/NW)

$V_{33}$. Net Sales to Fixed Assets (NS/FA)

$V_{34}$. Cash to Total Operating Expenditures (Cash interval ratio)

$V_{35}$. Defensive Assets to Total Operating Expenditures (Defensive interval ratio)

$V_{36}$. Defensive Assets Minus Current Liabilities to Total Operating Expenditures. (No Credit Interval ratio)

*Note:* The financial ratios from 1—36 are denoted by $V_1$, $V_2$, $V_3$,..., $V_{36}$.

### 3.2.2 *The Method of Analysis*

The analysis of data is grouped under two heads in order to verify the formulated hypotheses empirically:

(A) Univariate Analysis

(B) Multivariate Analysis

(A) *Univariate Analysis*

The basic object of univariate approach is to compare the financial ratios of failed companies with those of non-failed companies in order to detect systematic differences which might assist in predicting the chances of survival or failure of a company or companies. Under univariate approach, each ratio is considered individually for failed companies and non-failed companies. The analytical procedure applied for testing the hypotheses on univariate basis is based on:

1. **Comparison of Mean Values of Financial Ratios of Failed Companies and Non-Failed Companies**

The mean values of financial ratios are computed for the failed companies and non-failed companies in each of the years (i.e. upto a maximum of six years) prior to failure. The comparison of mean values of ratios for the two groups—failed group and non-failed group is undertaken in order to identify the discriminating power of ratios taken individually. It is not a predictive test. It is merely a convenient approach of sketching the general relationship between the failed and non-failed companies financial ratios. Student's t-values of each ratio is also computed in order to judge whether the difference between mean value of ratios of the two groups is statistically significant or insignificant.

2. **Dichotomous Classification Test**

The Dichotomous classification test predicts the failure status of a company based solely upon a knowledge of financial ratios. It is a simple predictive test measuring the relative differentiating power of various financial ratios. The classification test makes a dichotomous prediction i.e. a company is either classified into failed group or non-failed group. To make predictions of company failure, the ratios of mixed sample of failed and non-failed companies are arrayed i.e. each ratio is arrayed in ascending order marking the failed company with (X). The array of each ratio is inspected to find a best cut off point i.e. a point that minimises the percentage of classification error rates. The best cut off point is determined by trial and error process for each array separately. If the ratio of a company is below the cut off point, the company is classified as failed company. If the company's ratio is above the cut off point, it is classified as a non-failed company. If there are two cut off points in any array resulting in the same number of misclassification, anyone may be chosen, as our object is limited to the magnitude of classification error only. After classifying the each company either in one of the two groups, the predictions are compared with the actual status of companies in the sample and percentage of predictive accuracy is computed. The percentage of companies misclassified to the total number of companies in the array is indicative of degree of accuracy of the dichotomous classification test and is called a misclassification error. The ratio which shows the least percentage of misclassification over a period of six years prior to failure and the least misclassification at the earliest possible time (i.e. sixth year in our case) has the highest predictive power. This procedure is repeated for each of the 36 ratios.

It should, however, be noted that the univariate approach is a crude technique of predicting the chances of survival or failure of a company, because each ratio is considered individually and thus, indicates only the individual information value of a ratio. The ratios analysed and presented univariately are susceptible to faulty interpretations and may be confusing [31, p. 591]. The main shortcomings of univariate approach, as confirmed by few empirical studies [62-64, 80-83] are as under:

(1) the univariate approach ignores the interdependencies among the various ratios overtime which may exist on account of (a) some items in financial statement tend to move in the same direction as others, e.g. net income and dividends, sales and market costs; and (b) many ratios have common components e g. total sales in various activity ratios.

If, as the sparse evidence indicates, ratio distributions are substantially correlated overtime, then a smaller number of ratios taken together can convey the financial information contained in the financial statements.

(2) It may result in ambiguous inferences on account of conflicting signals, for instance, a firm with poor profitability ratio may be classified as a potential bankrupt, but, however, the situation may not be considered serious because of its high (i.e. above average) liquidity ratio.

Criticism levelled against univariate approach clearly brings out that financial ratios taken individually cannot provide the sufficient information for understanding the various economic dimensions of a company. A set of financial ratios may contain more useful information than any particular representative ratio. Therefore, the long list of ratios usually provided to users is substantially redundant.

Keeping in view the shortcomings of univariate approach, an attempt has been made to overcome its shortcomings by the use of multivariate analysis in which several ratios are combined into a model in order to predict the chances of survival or failure of a company.

(B) *Multivariate Analysis*

In multivariate analysis, several ratios are considered simultaneouly in order to develop an index or a meaningful predictive model. The construction of ratio index amounts to a formulation of a model designed to describe and predict the company failure. The formulation of failure prediction model involves specific problems which are to be considered:

(a) which ratios are most important and must be combined together in detecting the event i.e. company failure?
(b) what weights should be attached to the ratios in a certain combination? and
(c) how should the weights be objectively established?

After careful analysis of the nature and purpose of the study, statistical techniques known as Factor Analysis and Discriminant Analysis are applied to arrive at the final profile of ratios doing the best overall job together in the prediction of company failure. With the application of statistical techniques—Factor Analysis and Discriminant Analysis, the multivariate problem is actually reduced to a simple univariate problem and assignment of companies between two groups depends upon the value of a single variable. The following steps are taken to arrive at the final best discriminant function and to ascertain its predictive accuracy:

1. 36 variables (i.e. financial ratios) are screened and reduced to a smaller number of important variables having independent direction and uncorrelated with each other by using a statistical technique known as Factor Analysis.
2. Determination of relative weights to be attached to the variables determined under step-1 with the application of a statistical technique known as Discriminant Analysis.
3. Observation of predictive accuracy of various discriminant functions one year prior to the date of company failure;
4. Ascertaining the predictive accuracy of various discriminant functions one to six years prior to the date of company failure;
5. Determination of relative contributions of each independent variable to the total discriminating power of various ratio profiles with the use of scaled vector. The scaled vector is computed by multiplying corresponding variable coefficient by the square roots of the diagonal elements of the variance-covariance matrix; and
6. Selecting the final best discriminant function and determining the best cut off point.

The final best discriminant function and the best cut off point is that which results in the least percentage of misclassifications. It is this figure of percentage of classification error which forms the basis of selection of final best discriminant function. The discriminant function which results in the least percentage classification error over a period of six years prior to the date of failure and the least percentage of misclassification at the earliest possible time (i.e. sixth year) before failure, is selected as the final discriminant function performing the best job among the alternatives which include numerous computer runs analysing different ratio-profiles or discriminant functions.

7. The Discriminant Model is applied on a series of additional samples of companies taken irrespective of size, in a homogeneous and non-homogeneous groups in order to test the effectiveness of the model, as the real efficiency of the Discriminant Model lies in classifying those companies correctly which are not used to construct the best discriminant function.

### 3 2.3 *Statistical Techniques Applied for Model Development*

The statistical techniques which have been applied to analyse data and to built up a predictive model in order to verify the formulated hypotheses are outlined as under:

#### *Factor Analysis*

Factor analysis is a statistical technique of analysing a priori set of observations from their intercorrelations to determine whether the variations represented can be accounted for adequately by a number of basic characteristics smaller than that with which the investigation was started. Thus, data obtained with a large number of priori measures may be explained in terms of a smaller number of variables. Factor analysis, for this study, is chosen to reduce the number of variables (i.e. 36 ratios) by describing each linearly in terms of (n) new uncorrelated factors. The factor provides a parsimonious description of the observed data by retaining the most important information contained in the original data. The factor model extracts the maximum variance of the data explained by the underlying factors that described the structure and pattern of the original variables [84]. The number of factors are determined based on the criteria to extract and rotate factors with eigenvalues equal to or greater than 1. Since the eigenvalues measures the variance accounted for by a factor, this criteria assumes that the factors extracted define a certain level of variance among the variables. Since the variance of a variable is unity, the cut off rule rejects factors that do not account for at least the variance of one variable. In addition, a minimum loading of 0.40 of a variable on a factor used as an auxiliary criteria. Hofstede [85] chose a minimum factor load of 0.35, however, Rummel [86] chose a minimum factor load of 0.50. After careful analysis of the nature of problem, the factor analysis is chosen as an appropriate statistical technique for this study, because there is evidence [62-64] to believe that some of the ratios have a high degree of correlation with each other and the Factor analysis technique has the advantage of reducing the large number of variables (i.e. 36) to a smaller number of uncorrelated variables which will have the potentiality of conveying a great deal of information. Factor analysis basic assumption [87] which is found in financial ratios, is that, a battery of intercorrelated variables has common factors running through it and that the scores of individual variable can be represented more economically in terms of these reference factors. Secondly, the correlation between variables can be accounted for by the nature and extent of their factor loadings.

*Discriminant Analysis*

Discriminant Analysis is a statistical technique that classifies an observation into one of several *a priori* groupings on the basis of observation's individual characteristics under appropriate assumptions. The basic assumptions of Discriminant Analysis are as under:

(1) The n variables are normally distributed;
(2) the groups are discrete and known; and
(3) each observation in each group is described by a set of characteristics or variables.

It is used primarily for classification and/or making prediction in problems where the dependent variable appears in qualitative form e.g. good or bad; failed or non-failed; male or female. Therefore, the first step is to establish the groups explicitly as in this study two groups, namely, failed and non-failed are established. The number of original groups may be two or more. The purpose of discriminant function is to derive the linear combination of variables which best discriminate between the groups [88]. It attempts to determine the weights to be given to each of the original variables in order that the resulting composite score will have maximum potentiality for discriminating between the numbers of the two groups. In this manner, the multivariate problem is actually reduced to a simple univariate problem and the assignment of individuals between two groups depends upon the value of a single variable (i.e. combined score). To begin with, it is assumed that some unknown set of weighting coefficients exists which will define a composite score providing maximum discrimination between the two groups. The classification is done by means of a linear discriminant function and the desired discriminant function is, thus, of the form:

$$Y=\lambda_1 V_1 + \lambda_2 V_2 + \lambda_3 V_3 + \ldots + \lambda_n V_n$$

where $Y$=the discriminant score

$\lambda_1, \lambda_2, \lambda_3, \ldots, \lambda_n$ are the discriminant coefficients

$V_1, V_2, V_3, \ldots, V_n$ are discriminant variables.

The problem is to determine optimal values for the weighting coefficients such that the difference between mean scores for the two groups will be maximised relative to the variation within groups. The function to be maximised, as first defined by R.A. Fisher [89], is the ratio (i.e. F-ratio) between groups variance to the within groups variance. A test to determine the overall discriminating power of the model is the F-value which is the ratio of the sums of squares between groups to the sums-of-squares within-groups. When this ratio of the form,

$$F=\frac{(\bar{Y}_{g1}-\bar{Y}_{g2})^2}{\sum_{i=1}^{ng_1}(Y_i-\bar{Y}_{g1})^2+\sum_{i=1}^{ng_2}(Y_i-\bar{Y}_{g2})^2}$$

where

$(\bar{Y}_{g1}-\bar{Y}_{g2})^2$=Sum of squares of the difference between means of the two groups

$\sum_{i=1}^{ng_1}(Y_i-\bar{Y}_{g1})^2+\sum_{i=1}^{ng_2}(Y_i-\bar{Y}_{g2})^2$=the sum of squares within-groups is maximised, it has the effect of spreading the group means of Y-scores and simultaneously reducing the dispersion of individual scores around the group means. This test is appropriate because one of the objectives of discriminant analysis is to identify and to utilise those variables which best discriminate between groups and which are most similar within groups.

After careful analysis of the nature of problem and objective of the study, Discriminant Analysis is chosen as an appropriate statistical technique to classify the companies into one of the groups—failed group and non-failed group. Multiple Discriminant Analysis has been used in a variety of disciplines [90, 91, 92] since its first application in the 1930's by Fisher [89]. More recently this method has been applied in various empirical studies successfully in the area of finance specifically to the financial problems such as consumer credit evaluation and investment classification [93, 94], classification of high and low price earnings ratio firms [95], classification of firms into standard investment categories [96], and prediction of rate of return [97]. It has also been used with proven results for prediction of corporate failure in recent years by Altman [31, 32], Deakin [37] and Blum [39].

In the present study, financial ratios are used as discriminant variables and company failure as the predicted or dependent variable. There are only two groups—failed and non-failed, the analysis, therefore, takes the simplest form i.e. uni-dimensional. The discriminant analysis determines the discriminant coefficients of a set of variables (i.e. financial ratios) which do the best job of discriminating between failed companies and non-failed companies. When these coefficients are applied to actual ratios, a basis for classification into one of the mutually exclusive groupings exists. The discriminating power of the selected variables (i.e. ratios) profile is expressed by the classification error rates computed by the application of Y-scores and actual placement of the observations.

Discriminant analysis is chosen as an appropriate technique since it has the merit of considering an entire profile of ratios common to the relevant companies, as well as the interaction of these properties. A univariate study, on the other hand, can only consider the ratios used for group assignments one at a time. Secondly, it has the merit of yielding a model with a relatively small number of selected variables (i.e. ratios) which has the potential of conveying a great deal of information.

It is assumed for the application of Discriminant Analysis that financial ratios used as discriminatory variables are having normal distribution. This assumption is, however, based upon some of the empirical studies which concluded that financial ratios have normal distribution. Bird and McHugh [98] found in their study that the distribution of ratios within an industry can be approximated by a normal distribution in most of the cases, although quick asset structure ratios were often substantially non-normal at the significance level of=.05. Horrigan [62] has also suggested that financial ratios tend to be approximately normal. Deakin [99] has also found that with the exception of TD/TA ratio, most of the ratios are normally distributed.

## 3.3 **Accuracy and Validity of the Model**

The predictive accuracy of the discriminant model is ascertained by computing the percentage of classfication error over a period of six years prior to the date of failure in the initial sample. The misclassification rates are computed by comparing the predicted results of the discriminant model with the actual status of companies in the initial sample. The predictive accuracy of the model is considered in two dimensions:

Type I—The accuracy of correctly classifying the failed companies; and

Type II—The accuracy of correctly classifying non-failed companies.

A type I error would be predicting a failed company not to fail and a type II error would be predicting a non-failed company to fail. Various statistical significance tests such as Student's t-test, the common F-ratio test are conducted in order to judge the reliability of accuracy of the discriminant model. Student's t-test is applied to test the statistical significance of individual discriminating power of ratios and the common F-ratio, which is a transformation of the Mahalanobis measure of distance '$D^2$' is applied to test the statistical significance of the overall discriminating power of the model. '$D^2$' is the Mahalanobis squares distance between the centriods of the two groups. Statistical significance means that the results at a specified level, say, .01, are not obtained by chance alone.

In order to test the validity and effectiveness of the model rigorously, a series of additional samples of failed and non-failed companies are introduced and classification error rates over a period of six and three years are ascertained by using the parameters of the discriminant model established in the initial sample. The additional samples contain companies from both homogeneous and non-homogeneous group of industries. These samples are taken at random irrespective of size, fiscal year and age of the company. The importance of additional sample testing (i.e. validation tests) cannot be over-emphasized, since the real efficiency of the discriminant model lies in predicting the chances of survival or failure of a company or companies not contained in the initial sample, used to develop the parameters of the model.

Probabilities of misclassification of the best cut off point and the probability of individual company's belonging to each group is also computed in order to judge the predictive accuracy and validity of the discriminant model more rigorously in taking the classification decision between failed and non-failed companies with more confidence particularly in the cases of those individual companies whose discriminant scores lie near the cut off point and are more likely to be placed in the wrong group than those having extremely large or small discriminant scores.

## Chapter IV

# Testing the Hypotheses

### 4.0 Introduction

The core of the analysis in this chapter is regarding the empirical testing of the predictive power of a wide variety of financial ratios (refer Chapter III, pp. 53-54). The analysis and interpretation of the empirical results provide many insights into the strengths and weaknesses of different financial ratios and lead to the selection of a best set of ratios to predict company failure. The company failure predictive-capability of financial ratios has been judged by applying both the univariate and multivariate techniques.

The first section 4.1 attempts to test the statistical significance of the differences between the mean ratio values of the two groups, namely, failed group and non-failed group and depicts the predictive capability of financial ratios on univariate basis by the use of a technique known as Dichotomous Classification Test. The financial ratios have already been grouped broadly under profitability, solvency, liquidity and turnover ratios in Chapter III (pp. 53-54). Section 4.2 contains the description of arriving at a final best profile of ratios or the best discriminant function by using a multivariate technique, namely, Discriminant Analysis and also describes the empirical results arrived at for the prediction of company failure with the help of different combinations of financial ratios apart from the best set of ratios over a period of six years prior to company failure. The final section 4.3 shows the overall predictive performance of the discriminant model.

## 4.1 Empirical Findings-I: Univariate Analysis

In order to test the hypothesis:

$H_o$=Financial ratios used univariately cannot discriminate between the financial state of health of failed companies and non-failed companies.

On univariate basis, a univariate technique, namely, the Student's t-test has been applied for testing the statistical significance of the difference between the mean values of the two groups, namely, failed group and non-failed group. The method involved in calculation and the findings are under the heads given below:

### 4.1.1 *T-test of Significance of Difference between the Mean Values of Ratios of Failed Companies and Non-Failed Companies.*

The purpose of comparison of mean values of ratios is to detect the systematic differences and to judge the general relationship between the financial ratios of failed companies and non-failed companies. But the comparison of the mean values of ratios of failed companies and non-failed companies does not reflect the statistical significance of the mean difference. Student's t-test, therefore, has been applied to measure whether the difference between the mean values of 36 financial ratios of failed companies and non-failed companies is statistically significant and thus, to test the individual discriminating power of financial ratios between the state of financial health of failed companies and non-failed companies. The 't' values of 36 financial ratios have been computed by the Statistical Analysis System (SAS) of IBM 360/44 computer at the Delhi University Computer Centre, Delhi. The 't' values of each ratio is computed by a formula given below:

$$\text{'T'} = \frac{\bar{V}_{g1i} - \bar{V}_{g2i}}{S} \times \sqrt{\frac{n_1 n_2}{n_1 + n_2}}$$

where

$\bar{V}_{g1i}$=mean of ith variable of group 1

$\bar{V}_{g2i}$=mean of ith variable of group 2

$n_1$ = number of observations in group 1

$n_2$ = number of observations in group 2

$S$ = combined standard deviation.

The value of S is calculated as follows:

$$S=\sqrt{\frac{\Sigma(\bar{V}_{g1i}-V_{g1i})^2+\Sigma(\bar{V}_{g2i}-V_{g2i})^2}{n_1+n_2-2}}$$

where

$(\bar{V}_{g1i}-V_{g1i})^2$ = squares of deviation of the original scores (ith variable) from the mean of ith variable of group 1

$(\bar{V}_{g2i}-V_{g2i})^2$ = squares of deviation of the original scores (ith variable) from mean of ith variable of group 2.

If the calculated value of '$t$' is greater than the table value at .05 (.01) level of significance [i.e. '$t$' > $t_{0\cdot 05}$ ($t_{0\cdot 01}$)], the difference between the ratios of group means will be considered significant at 5% (1%) level of significance and the hypothesis will be rejected and *vice-versa*.

The mean values of 36 ratios of both the groups, their respective mean differences, combined standard deviations and finally t-values are worked out with the help of computer and presented below in Table 4-1.

TABLE 4-1. **Mean and T-Values of Ratios for the Two Groups One Year Prior to Failure**

| Ratio | Group 1 Means | Group 2 Means | t-values |
|---|---|---|---|
| I. *Profitability Ratios* | | | |
| (a) *Cash Flow Ratios* | | | |
| $V_1$—CF/NS | —0.7752 | 0.0538 | 2.24* |
| $V_2$—CF/TTA | —0.1315 | 0.0746 | 7.72 |
| $V_3$—CF/NW | —0.9399 | 0.2347 | 3.57 |
| $V_4$—CF/TD | —0.0867 | 0.1477 | 5.59 |

TABLE 4-1 (*Contd.*)

| Ratio | Group 1 Means | Group 2 Means | t-values |
|---|---|---|---|
| (b) *Income Ratios* | | | |
| $V_5$—NI/NS | --0.9693 | 0.0447 | 2.39* |
| $V_6$—NI/TTA | —0.1476 | 0.0449 | 6.32 |
| $V_7$—NI/NW | —0.9991 | 0.1317 | 3.05 |
| $V_8$—NI/TD | —0.9646 | 0.0941 | 1.25** |
| $V_9$—EBIT/TTA | —0.0938 | 0.1198 | 9.34 |
| $V_{10}$—EBIT/NS | —0.5465 | 0.0870 | 2.37* |
| $V_{11}$—NOP/NS | —0.6586 | 0.0767 | 1.99** |
| $V_{12}$—EBIT/Int | —2.2888 | 3.3656 | 5.04 |
| $V_{13}$—NI/NWC | —0.9024 | 0 3157 | 4.38 |
| II. *Solvency Ratios* | | | |
| $V_{14}$—TTA/CD | 3.5222 | 2.1097 | 2.12* |
| $V_{15}$—TTA/LTD | 2.0688 | 5.7535 | 2.37** |
| $V_{16}$—TTA/TD | 1.3202 | 1.6479 | 1.21** |
| $V_{17}$—NW/TD | 0.3710 | 0.6427 | 0.96** |
| $V_{18}$—NW/LTD | 0.3108 | 1.7095 | 2.43* |
| III. *Liquidity Ratios* | | | |
| (a) *Liquid Assets to TTA Ratios* | | | |
| $V_{19}$—C/TTA | 0.0710 | 0.0402 | 0.98** |
| $V_{20}$—QA/TTA | 0.2907 | 0.3229 | 0.63** |
| $V_{21}$—CA/TTA | 0.5563 | 0.7198 | 3.12 |
| $V_{22}$—NWC/TTA | 0.0630 | 0.1605 | 1.03* |
| (b) *Liquid Assets to CD Ratios* | | | |
| $V_{23}$—C/CL | 0.9476 | 0.1319 | 1.26** |
| $V_{24}$—QA/CL | 0.6935 | 2.7311 | 1.25** |
| $V_{25}$—CA/CL | 1.4426 | 3.3969 | 1.22** |

| Ratio | Group 1 Means | Group 2 Means | t-values |
|---|---|---|---|
| IV. *Turnover Ratios* | | | |
| $V_{26}$—NS/Debtors | 7.0704 | 11.5271 | 1.31** |
| $V_{27}$—NS/Inv. | 1.5309 | 4.6512 | 3.94 |
| $V_{28}$—NS/QA | 4.8542 | 6.7260 | 1.33** |
| $V_{29}$—NS/CA | 1.9696 | 2.5870 | 0.87** |
| $V_{30}$—NS/NWC | 0.3593 | 12.0122 | 5.77 |
| $V_{31}$—NS/TTA | 0.6128 | 1.8591 | 4.43 |
| $V_{32}$—NS/NW | 1.9334 | 6.4914 | 2.92 |
| $V_{33}$—C/TOE (Cash Interval Ratio) | 0.4762 | 0.0284 | 1.27** |
| $V_{35}$—DA/TOE (Defensive Interval Ratio) | 0.2821 | 0.8171 | 1.49** |
| $V_{36}$—DA-CL/TOE (No credit interval ratio) | —01.5597 | —0.1996 | 1.46** |

*Notes*: $V_{1-36}$ denote the variables.
Group 1 represents the failed companies
Group 2 represents the non-failed companies
$t_{1,76}$ (.01)=2.64
$t_{1,76}$ (.05)=1.99
*denotes insignificant at .01 level
**denote insignificant at .05 level.

The analysis of Table 4-1 clearly indicates that the difference between the mean values of 21 ratios given below is significant at .05 level of significance:

I. *Profitability Ratios*

| | |
|---|---|
| $V_1$-CF/NS | $V_7$-NI/NW |
| $V_2$-CF/TTA | $V_9$ -EBIT/TTA |
| $V_3$-CF/NW | $V_{10}$-EBIT/NS |

$V_4$-CF/TD
$V_5$-NI/NS
$V_6$-NI/TTA
$V_{11}$-NOP/NS
$V_{12}$-EBIT/Int.
$V_{13}$-NI/NWC

II. *Solvency Ratios*

$V_{14}$-TTA/CD
$V_{15}$-TTA/LTD
$V_{16}$-NW/LTD

III. *Liquidity Ratios*

$V_{21}$-CA/TTA

IV. *Turnover Ratios*

$V_{27}$-NS/Inv.
$V_{30}$-NS/NWC
$V_{31}$-NS/TTA
$V_{32}$-NS/NW
$V_{33}$-NS/FA

The 't'-value of the above mentioned 21 ratios is greater than the tabulated T-value (i.e. 1.99 for $t_{1,76}$ (.05) level of significance), hence, the null hypothesis (i.e. $H_0$) is rejected in the case of 21 financial ratios. It is, therefore, contended that the 21 ratios can discriminate between the financial state of health of two groups, namely, failed group and non-failed group. The null hypothesis is not rejected in the case of 15 financial ratios given below, since the 't'-values of these ratios is smaller than the tabulated t-value:

I. *Profitability Ratios*

$V_8$ -NI/TD

II. *Solvency Ratios*

$V_{16}$-TA/TD
$V_{17}$-NW/TD

III. *Liquidity Ratios*

$V_{19}$-C/TTA
$V_{20}$-QA/TTA
$V_{22}$-NWC/TTA
$V_{23}$-C/CL
$V_{24}$-QA/CL
$V_{25}$-CA/CL

IV *Turnover Ratios*

$V_{26}$–NS/Debtors
$V_{28}$–NS/QA
$V_{29}$–NS/CA
$V_{34}$–C/TOE
$V_{35}$–DA/TOE
$V_{36}$–DA·CL/TOE

The above results lead to conclude that the solvency, liquidity and liquidity turnover ratios' mean differences are not significant at $t_{1,78}$ (.01) and $t_{1,76}$ (.05) level of significance, hence, not significant variables to discriminate between the two groups. Profitability ratios and turnover ratios (except liquidity turnover) are significant variables in discriminating between the two groups on univariate basis. Among profitability ratios $V_9$ i.e. EBIT/TTA is the most significant ratio followed by CF/TTA and NI/TTA in discriminating between the two groups on individual basis.

Liquidity variables are the least significant variables in discriminating between the financial health of two groups, namely, failed group and non-failed group. There can be several explanations for the poor showing of liquidity ratios e.g. to some extent it could be attributed to 'Window-dressing' by management as the company approaches towards failure.

The Student's t-test indicates the difference and the statistical significance of difference between the mean values of ratios of failed companies and non-failed companies, but does not speak anything about the predictive power of ratios. To test the predictive capability of ratios on univariate basis a technique known as 'Dichotomous Classification Test' has been applied.

### 4.1.2 *Dichotomous Classification Test*

To test the hypothesis:

$H_0$=Financial ratios used univariately cannot predict the chances of survival or failure of a company or companies.

a technique called 'dichotomous classification test' has been applied which predicts the failure status of a company based solely upon a knowledge of the financial ratios. Under the dichotomous classification test, an optimal cut off point for each ratio is established which classifies the observations with minimum error of classification. In this study, thirty six ratios are computed and arrayed in ascending order for each of the six years prior to failure for each firm in the sample (i.e. 39 failed firms and 39 non-failed firms). The percentage classification error for each of the 36 financial ratios for six years before failure is shown below in Table 4-2.

TABLE 4-2. **Percentage Error for 36 Financial Ratios on Dichotomous Classification Test**

| Ratio | Year Before Failure | | | | | |
|---|---|---|---|---|---|---|
| | 1 | 2 | 3 | 4 | 5 | 6 |
| I. *Profitability Ratios* | | | | | | |
| (a) *Cash Flow Ratios* | | | | | | |
| $V_1$—CF/NS | 11 | 22 | 18 | 27 | 30 | 31 |
| $V_2$—CF/TTA | 10 | 16 | 19 | 23 | 28 | 28 |
| $V_3$—CF/NW | 11 | 15 | 19 | 24 | 28 | 29 |
| $V_4$—CF/TD | 13 | 18 | 18 | 23 | 29 | 30 |
| (b) *Income Ratios* | | | | | | |
| $V_5$—NI/NS | 14 | 19 | 18 | 30 | 32 | 31 |
| $V_6$—NI/TTA | 13 | 17 | 18 | 23 | 29 | 29 |
| $V_7$—NI/NW | 13 | 16 | 17 | 24 | 31 | 33 |
| $V_8$—NI/TD | 13 | 19 | 17 | 25 | 33 | 34 |
| $V_9$—EBIT/TTA | 10 | 17 | 17 | 24 | 29 | 29 |
| $V_{10}$—EBIT/NS | 15 | 19 | 20 | 25 | 31 | 35 |
| $V_{11}$—NOP/NS | 16 | 22 | 23 | 27 | 28 | 32 |
| $V_{12}$—EBIT/Int. | 14 | 16 | 17 | 25 | 29 | 31 |
| $V_{13}$—NI/NWC | 14 | 21 | 24 | 27 | 30 | 33 |
| II. *Solvency Ratios* | | | | | | |
| $V_{14}$—TTA/CD | 41 | 40 | 55 | 53 | 52 | 54 |
| $V_{15}$—TTA/LTD | 15 | 19 | 21 | 28 | 32 | 35 |
| $V_{16}$—TTA/TD | 18 | 23 | 26 | 31 | 33 | 36 |

| Ratio | Year Before Failure | | | | | |
|---|---|---|---|---|---|---|
| | 1 | 2 | 3 | 4 | 5 | 6 |
| $V_{17}$—NW/TD | 18 | 26 | 30 | 35 | 38 | 42 |
| $V_{18}$—NW/LTD | 14 | 21 | 22 | 28 | 32 | 35 |
| III. *Liquidity Ratios* | | | | | | |
| (a) *Liquid Assets to TTA Ratios* | | | | | | |
| $V_{19}$—C/TTA | 35 | 46 | 49 | 48 | 46 | 47 |
| $V_{20}$—QA/TTA | 37 | 35 | 38 | 42 | 45 | 46 |
| $V_{21}$—CA/TTA | 32 | 33 | 32 | 37 | 39 | 41 |
| $V_{22}$—NWC/TTA | 35 | 41 | 40 | 45 | 47 | 48 |
| (b) *Liquid Assets to Current Debt Ratios* | | | | | | |
| $V_{23}$—C/CL | 36 | 46 | 51 | 50 | 52 | 49 |
| $V_{24}$—QA/CL | 35 | 38 | 43 | 45 | 46 | 47 |
| $V_{25}$—CA/CL | 33 | 37 | 39 | 45 | 44 | 46 |
| IV. *Turnover Ratios* | | | | | | |
| $V_{26}$—NS/Debtors | 29 | 27 | 33 | 35 | 37 | 39 |
| $V_{27}$—NS/Inv. | 19 | 17 | 25 | 29 | 31 | 35 |
| $V_{28}$—NS QA | 26 | 27 | 33 | 36 | 37 | 39 |
| $V_{29}$—NS/CA | 23 | 22 | 32 | 35 | 36 | 37 |
| $V_{30}$—NS/NWC | 13 | 22 | 29 | 31 | 32 | 32 |
| $V_{31}$—NS/TTA | 20 | 21 | 24 | 26 | 33 | 35 |
| $V_{32}$—NS/NW | 13 | 17 | 21 | 37 | 31 | 33 |
| $V_{33}$—NS/FA | 23 | 22 | 23 | 28 | 32 | 35 |
| $V_{34}$—Cash Interval Ratio | 36 | 46 | 51 | 55 | 52 | 49 |
| $V_{35}$—Defensive Interval Ratio | 41 | 47 | 45 | 48 | 49 | 51 |
| $V_{36}$—No Credit Interval Ratio | 35 | 34 | 41 | 42 | 45 | 49 |

The empirical results in Table 4-2 clearly illustrate the superiority of profitability ratios in predicting the corporate failure. From Table 4-2, it is evident that the cash-flow to total tangible assets ratio possesses the highest predictive power followed by the earning before interest and taxes to total tangible assets ratio. In the first year before failure, the classification error of $V_2$ (CF/TTA) and $V_9$ (EBIT/TTA) is 10 per cent and 10 per cent respectively, while in the sixth year, the error percentages are 28 and 29 respectively. Both error percentages are much smaller than would be expected from a random prediction model, where the expected percentage error would be approximately 50 per cent. The turnover ratios show somewhat inferior results than the profitability ratios in predicting corporate health.

The predictive accuracy of all solvency and liquidity ratios is found to be much less than that of profitability and turnover ratios. Among the solvency and liquidity ratios, solvency ratios are found more reliable predictor of corporate health than the liquidity ratios. The solvency ratios directly or indirectly measure the reliance of a company on debt. The empirical results indicate that companies with heavy debt and inadequate equity base are more prone to failure/sickness. The classification error of solvency ratios clearly show that there is a definite association between the incidence of failure and inadequacy of equity base.

The classification error shown in Table 4-2 clearly indicate that the predictive power of all the liquidity ratios is quite poor. The current ratio ($V_{25}$) and the quick ratio ($V_{24}$) result in almost three and a half times more classification error than the best profitability ratio. These empirical results contradict the considerable importance traditionally attached to liquidity ratios in appraising corporate health and hence, the great importance attached to the liquidity ratios, especially to the current ratio and quick ratio, seems to be ill founded. All other liquidity ratios also show poor results. This implies that the liquidity ratios are not of much use in detecting the corporate failure.

The above analysis leads to conclude that the financial ratios possess predictive power and can predict the potential corporate failure/sickness used on univariate basis. But not all ratios predict equally well. There is a relative difference in the predictive power of financial ratios. The cash-flow to total tangible assets ratio has the ability to correctly classify both the failed and non-failed firms to a much greater extent throughout the six years period before failure than would be possible through random prediction. However, the predictive power of liquidity ratios is much lower. Secondly, the net cash flow supplied to the reservoir is the most crucial factor, while the size of the reservoir is the least important factor in detecting the potential corporate failure/sickness.

## 4.2 **Empirical Findings—II: Multivariate Analysis**

After analysis and recognition of the discriminating and predictive power of financial ratios on univariate basis and its limitations (refer Chapter III, pp. 93-94) to predict the event i.e. company failure, an attempt has been made to test the undermentioned hypotheses on the basis of multivariate analysis which attempts to derive a linear combination of financial characteristics (i.e. ratios) which best discriminate between the groups, namely, failed group and non-failed group of companies:

(1) $H_0$=Financial ratios used multivariately cannot predict the chances of survival or failure of a company or companies.

(2) $H_0$=There is no relative difference in the predictive power of financial ratios in discriminating between the failed companies and non-failed companies.

In multivariate approach, several financial ratios are taken simultaneously and an index or a model is developed which measures both (a) an operational aspect which is highly sensitive to changes in the general health of the enterprise and (b) the firm's reserve strength available to bear shocks arising from unexpected set backs, managerial errors or external factors. Both the aspects i.e. operational and reserve strength of a company are analysed by taking profitability and balance sheet ratios simultaneously in different combinations, explaining the event of failure/bankruptcy.

### 4.2.1 *Model Development*

From the original list of 36 financial ratios, four variables are selected as the ones which have better discriminating power and thus, contribute most towards the prediction of chances of survival or failure/bankruptcy of a company. In order to arrive at a best discriminant function consisting of four variables, the following steps have been taken:

I. Reduction of variables to a smaller number of variables having independent direction and uncorrelated with each other by the use of factor analysis;
II. Evaluation of intercorrelations between the relevant variables;
III. Formation of various profiles of ratios and observation of the predictive accuracy measured in terms of classification error rates of the various ratio-profiles by the use of a statistical technique known as discriminant analysis; and
IV. Observation of the overall predictive accuracy (i.e. accuracy over a period of six years prior to failure of the various discriminant functions and selecting the best discriminant function i.e. the discriminant function which discriminates between failed group and non-failed group with least classification error rates.

First of all, 36 variables (financial ratios) were computed for each of the failed and non-failed companies in the initial sample from the financial statements one year prior to failure. The intercorrelations between the 36 variables of both the groups, namely, failed group and non-failed group were factorially analysed using the principal components method of Factor Analysis. Factor Analysis was carried out on IBM 360/44 computer system available at Delhi University Computer Centre, Delhi.

The solution produced:

(i) The factor matrix before rotation;
(ii) the rotated factor matrix;
(iii) the eigenvalues of each factor and the percentage of total variance in the data explained by each factor (Appendix L); and

(iv) the factor loading of each variable on a factor. Factor loading is equal to the correlation coefficient between a variable and a factor. In factor analysis, factor loadings indicate the cluster of variables on a factor.

From the rotated matrix, ten factors in group-1 and eight factors in group-2 accounting for 84.2 per cent and 86.1 per cent respectively of the total variance in the data were extracted. The variables found to load 0.40 or higher on a factor were selected as its domain in both the groups. There was no evidence of a single general factor accounting for a large percentage of variations in the data. The contribution of each factor ranged from 21.9 per cent to 2.9 per cent in group-1 and 30 per cent to 2.9 in group-2. The factors, the variables clustered on each factor and their loading are shown in Table 4-3.

TABLE 4-3. **Rotated Factor Loading (0.40 and above) Pattern of Variables Extracted from the Rotated Factor Matrix**

| Group—1 | | | Group—2 | | |
|---|---|---|---|---|---|
| Factor | Variable | Loading | Factor | Variable | Loading |
| $F_1$ | $V_{16}$ | .797 | $F_1$ | $V_2$ | .741 |
| | $V_{17}$ | .843 | | $V_4$ | .957 |
| | $V_{18}$ | .647 | | $V_6$ | .655 |
| | $V_{23}$ | .971 | | $V_8$ | .923 |
| | $V_{24}$ | .970 | | $V_9$ | .488 |
| | $V_{25}$ | .969 | | $V_{14}$ | .633 |
| $F_2$ | $V_{26}$ | .832 | | $V_{16}$ | .923 |
| | $V_{27}$ | .494 | | $V_{17}$ | .925 |
| | $V_{28}$ | .716 | | $V_{19}$ | .895 |
| | $V_{31}$ | .794 | | $V_{23}$ | .957 |
| | $V_{32}$ | .774 | | $V_{24}$ | .789 |
| | $V_{33}$ | .866 | | $V_{25}$ | .622 |
| | | | | $V_{29}$ | .707 |
| | | | | $V_{31}$ | .591 |

TABLE 4-3 (*Contd.*)

| Group—1 | | | Group—2 | | |
|---|---|---|---|---|---|
| Factor | Variable | Loading | Factor | Variable | Loading |
| $F_3$ | $V_2$ | .907 | $F_2$ | $V_1$ | .860 |
| | $V_4$ | .649 | | $V_{10}$ | .929 |
| | $V_6$ | .897 | | $V_{11}$ | .870 |
| | $V_9$ | .873 | | $V_{21}$ | —.515 |
| | $V_{13}$ | .459 | | $V_{29}$ | —.459 |
| | | | | $V_{30}$ | —.479 |
| $F_4$ | $V_{15}$ | —.413 | | $V_{31}$ | .545 |
| | $V_{19}$ | .506 | | $V_{32}$ | .780 |
| | $V_{34}$ | .948 | | $V_{33}$ | .457 |
| | $V_{35}$ | .951 | | $V_{35}$ | .473 |
| $F_5$ | $V_1$ | .558 | $F_3$ | $V_2$ | .535 |
| | $V_5$ | .700 | | $V_3$ | .863 |
| | $V_{10}$ | .958 | | $V_4$ | .626 |
| | $V_{11}$ | .958 | | $V_6$ | .619 |
| | | | | $V_7$ | .843 |
| $F_6$ | $V_{15}$ | .465 | | $V_9$ | .584 |
| | $V_{18}$ | .509 | | $V_{13}$ | .671 |
| | $V_{20}$ | .638 | | $V_{30}$ | .442 |
| | $V_{21}$ | .773 | | | |
| | $V_{22}$ | .719 | $F_4$ | $V_{20}$ | .707 |
| | $V_{28}$ | —.440 | | $V_{21}$ | .515 |
| | $V_{29}$ | —.703 | | $V_{26}$ | —.695 |
| | $V_{36}$ | .506 | | $V_{28}$ | —.665 |
| | | | | $V_{35}$ | .448 |
| $F_7$ | $V_3$ | .886 | $F_5$ | $V_{12}$ | .779 |
| | $V_7$ | .875 | | $V_{27}$ | .830 |
| | | | | $V_{29}$ | .449 |
| $F_8$ | $V_{14}$ | .806 | | $V_{31}$ | .526 |
| | $V_{36}$ | .440 | | $V_{33}$ | .583 |

| | Group—1 | | | Group—2 | |
|---|---|---|---|---|---|
| Factor | Variable | Loading | Factor | Variable | Loading |
| $F_9$ | $V_1$ | .783 | $F_6$ | $V_{15}$ | .925 |
| | $V_5$ | .670 | | $V_{18}$ | .937 |
| | $V_{12}$ | .929 | $F_7$ | $V_{14}$ | .538 |
| $F_{10}$ | $V_8$ | .646 | | $V_{22}$ | .809 |
| | $V_{30}$ | .497 | | $V_{24}$ | .481 |
| | | | | $V_{25}$ | .696 |
| | | | | $V_{36}$ | .832 |
| | | | $F_8$ | $V_{13}$ | —.476 |
| | | | | $V_{34}$ | .620 |
| | | | | $V_{35}$ | .497 |

*Notes:* 1. Group-1 represents failed companies
Group-2 represents non-failed companies
2. F denotes factor
V denotes variables.

Fifteen variables clustering around five factors were extracted from the above Table 4-3 based on the criterion:

(a) Factor loading of a variable;
(b) a variable or variables loaded on the same factor in both the groups; and
(c) the observation of correlation within the variables clustering around a factor.

The number of factors, the variables clustered on each factor and their loading are presented in Table 4-4.

The analysis of the factors given in Table 4-4 shows that (a) two factors ($F_4$ and $F_6$) are loaded with only one variable on each, (b) one factor i.e. $F_2$ is loaded with three variables; and the remaining two factors i.e. $F_1$, $F_3$ are loaded with five variables on each.

Initially seventy five ratio-profiles consisting of five variables each were formulated and their predictive accuracy

TABLE 4-4. **Factor Loading Pattern of Variables Extracted from the above Table 4-3**

| Factor | Variable | Loading | |
|---|---|---|---|
| | | Group-1 | Group-2 |
| $F_1$ | $V_{16}$ | .797 | .923 |
| | $V_{17}$ | .843 | .925 |
| | $V_{23}$ | .970 | .957 |
| | $V_{24}$ | .971 | .789 |
| | $V_{25}$ | .969 | .622 |
| $F_2$ | $V_{31}$ | .794 | .595 |
| | $V_{32}$ | .774 | .780 |
| | $V_{33}$ | .866 | .457 |
| $F_3$ | $V_2$ | .907 | .535 |
| | $V_4$ | .649 | .624 |
| | $V_6$ | .897 | .619 |
| | $V_9$ | .873 | .584 |
| | $V_{13}$ | .459 | .671 |
| $F_4$ | $V_{35}$ | .951 | .448 |
| $F_6$ | $V_{15}$ | .465 | .925 |

one year prior to failure was ascertained by the use of a statistical technique known as discriminant analysis. Apart from the above, twenty four ratio-profiles were also formulated by adding or deleting variables in the list of fifteen variables loaded on five factors and their predictive accuracy was computed. The discriminant functions were carried out on IBM 360/44 computer available at the Computer Centre, University of Delhi. The variables in various discriminant functions and their predictive accuracy i.e. percentage of correctly classifying the companies in the sample are shown in Table 4-5.

TABLE 4-5. **Predictive Accuracy of 99 Discriminant Functions One Year Prior to Failure**

| S. No. | Variables | Number of Variables | Percentage Correctly Classified |
|---|---|---|---|
| 1. | $V_2$ $V_{15}$ $V_{16}$ $V_{31}$ $V_{35}$ | 5 | 90 |
| 2. | $V_2$ $V_{15}$ $V_{16}$ $V_{32}$ $V_{35}$ | 5 | 91 |
| 3. | $V_2$ $V_{15}$ $V_{16}$ $V_{33}$ $V_{35}$ | 5 | 86 |
| 4. | $V_4$ $V_{15}$ $V_{16}$ $V_{31}$ $V_{35}$ | 5 | 82 |
| 5. | $V_4$ $V_{15}$ $V_{16}$ $V_{32}$ $V_{35}$ | 5 | 65 |
| 6. | $V_4$ $V_{15}$ $V_{16}$ $V_{33}$ $V_{35}$ | 5 | 63 |
| 7. | $V_6$ $V_{15}$ $V_{16}$ $V_{31}$ $V_{35}$ | 5 | 90 |
| 8. | $V_6$ $V_{15}$ $V_{16}$ $V_{32}$ $V_{35}$ | 5 | 86 |
| 9. | $V_6$ $V_{15}$ $V_{16}$ $V_{33}$ $V_{35}$ | 5 | 82 |
| 10. | $V_9$ $V_{15}$ $V_{16}$ $V_{31}$ $V_{35}$ | 5 | 94* |
| 11. | $V_9$ $V_{15}$ $V_{16}$ $V_{32}$ $V_{35}$ | 5 | 91 |
| 12. | $V_9$ $V_{15}$ $V_{16}$ $V_{33}$ $V_{35}$ | 5 | 90 |
| 13. | $V_{13}$ $V_{15}$ $V_{16}$ $V_{31}$ $V_{35}$ | 5 | 82 |
| 14. | $V_{13}$ $V_{15}$ $V_{16}$ $V_{32}$ $V_{35}$ | 5 | 65 |
| 15. | $V_{13}$ $V_{15}$ $V_{16}$ $V_{33}$ $V_{35}$ | 5 | 58 |
| 16. | $V_2$ $V_{15}$ $V_{17}$ $V_{31}$ $V_{35}$ | 5 | 91 |
| 17. | $V_2$ $V_{15}$ $V_{17}$ $V_{32}$ $V_{35}$ | 5 | 86 |
| 18. | $V_2$ $V_{15}$ $V_{17}$ $V_{33}$ $V_{35}$ | 5 | 75 |
| 19. | $V_4$ $V_{15}$ $V_{17}$ $V_{31}$ $V_{35}$ | 5 | 67 |
| 20. | $V_4$ $V_{15}$ $V_{17}$ $V_{32}$ $V_{35}$ | 5 | 60 |
| 21. | $V_4$ $V_{15}$ $V_{17}$ $V_{33}$ $V_{35}$ | 5 | 56 |
| 22. | $V_6$ $V_{15}$ $V_{17}$ $V_{31}$ $V_{35}$ | 5 | 91 |
| 23. | $V_6$ $V_{15}$ $V_{17}$ $V_{32}$ $V_{35}$ | 5 | 86 |
| 24. | $V_6$ $V_{15}$ $V_{17}$ $V_{33}$ $V_{35}$ | 5 | 74 |
| 25. | $V_9$ $V_{15}$ $V_{17}$ $V_{31}$ $V_{35}$ | 5 | 93* |
| 26. | $V_9$ $V_{15}$ $V_{17}$ $V_{32}$ $V_{35}$ | 5 | 85 |
| 27. | $V_9$ $V_{15}$ $V_{17}$ $V_{33}$ $V_{35}$ | 5 | 73 |
| 28. | $V_{13}$ $V_{15}$ $V_{17}$ $V_{31}$ $V_{35}$ | 5 | 74 |

TABLE 4-5 (*Contd.*)

| S. No. | Variables | Number of Variables | Percentage Correctly Classified |
|---|---|---|---|
| 29. | $V_{13}$ $V_{15}$ $V_{17}$ $V_{32}$ $V_{35}$ | 5 | 63 |
| 30. | $V_{13}$ $V_{15}$ $V_{17}$ $V_{33}$ $V_{35}$ | 5 | 57 |
| 31. | $V_{2}$ $V_{15}$ $V_{23}$ $V_{31}$ $V_{35}$ | 5 | 87 |
| 32. | $V_{2}$ $V_{15}$ $V_{23}$ $V_{32}$ $V_{35}$ | 5 | 82 |
| 33. | $V_{2}$ $V_{15}$ $V_{23}$ $V_{33}$ $V_{35}$ | 5 | 73 |
| 34. | $V_{4}$ $V_{15}$ $V_{23}$ $V_{31}$ $V_{35}$ | 5 | 59 |
| 35. | $V_{4}$ $V_{15}$ $V_{23}$ $V_{32}$ $V_{35}$ | 5 | 51 |
| 36. | $V_{4}$ $V_{15}$ $V_{23}$ $V_{33}$ $V_{35}$ | 5 | 51 |
| 37. | $V_{6}$ $V_{15}$ $V_{23}$ $V_{31}$ $V_{35}$ | 5 | 91 |
| 38. | $V_{6}$ $V_{25}$ $V_{23}$ $V_{32}$ $V_{35}$ | 5 | 86 |
| 39. | $V_{6}$ $V_{15}$ $V_{23}$ $V_{33}$ $V_{35}$ | 5 | 74 |
| 40. | $V_{9}$ $V_{15}$ $V_{23}$ $V_{31}$ $V_{35}$ | 5 | 93* |
| 41. | $V_{9}$ $V_{15}$ $V_{23}$ $V_{32}$ $V_{35}$ | 5 | 90 |
| 42. | $V_{9}$ $V_{15}$ $V_{23}$ $V_{33}$ $V_{35}$ | 5 | 74 |
| 43. | $V_{13}$ $V_{15}$ $V_{23}$ $V_{31}$ $V_{35}$ | 5 | 70 |
| 44. | $V_{13}$ $V_{15}$ $V_{23}$ $V_{32}$ $V_{35}$ | 5 | 68 |
| 45. | $V_{13}$ $V_{15}$ $V_{23}$ $V_{33}$ $V_{35}$ | 5 | 62 |
| 46. | $V_{2}$ $V_{15}$ $V_{24}$ $V_{31}$ $V_{35}$ | 5 | 92 |
| 47. | $V_{2}$ $V_{15}$ $V_{24}$ $V_{32}$ $V_{35}$ | 5 | 86 |
| 48. | $V_{2}$ $V_{15}$ $V_{24}$ $V_{33}$ $V_{35}$ | 5 | 78 |
| 49. | $V_{4}$ $V_{15}$ $V_{24}$ $V_{31}$ $V_{35}$ | 5 | 80 |
| 50. | $V_{4}$ $V_{15}$ $V_{24}$ $V_{32}$ $V_{35}$ | 5 | 64 |
| 51. | $V_{4}$ $V_{15}$ $V_{24}$ $V_{33}$ $V_{35}$ | 5 | 64 |
| 52. | $V_{6}$ $V_{15}$ $V_{24}$ $V_{31}$ $V_{35}$ | 5 | 91 |
| 53. | $V_{6}$ $V_{15}$ $V_{24}$ $V_{32}$ $V_{35}$ | 5 | 86 |
| 54. | $V_{6}$ $V_{15}$ $V_{24}$ $V_{33}$ $V_{35}$ | 5 | 83 |
| 55. | $V_{9}$ $V_{15}$ $V_{24}$ $V_{31}$ $V_{35}$ | 5 | 93* |
| 56. | $V_{9}$ $V_{15}$ $V_{24}$ $V_{32}$ $V_{35}$ | 5 | 90 |

| S. No. | Variables | Number of Variables | Percentage Correctly Classified |
|---|---|---|---|
| 57. | $V_9$ $V_{15}$ $V_{24}$ $V_{33}$ $V_{35}$ | 5 | 81 |
| 58. | $V_{13}$ $V_{15}$ $V_{24}$ $V_{31}$ $V_{35}$ | 5 | 82 |
| 59. | $V_{13}$ $V_{15}$ $V_{24}$ $V_{32}$ $V_{35}$ | 5 | 60 |
| 60. | $V_{13}$ $V_{15}$ $V_{24}$ $V_{33}$ $V_{35}$ | 5 | 62 |
| 61. | $V_2$ $V_{15}$ $V_{25}$ $V_{31}$ $V_{35}$ | 5 | 94* |
| 62. | $V_2$ $V_{15}$ $V_{25}$ $V_{32}$ $V_{35}$ | 5 | 86 |
| 63. | $V_2$ $V_{15}$ $V_{25}$ $V_{33}$ $V_{35}$ | 5 | 85 |
| 64. | $V_4$ $V_{15}$ $V_{25}$ $V_{31}$ $V_{35}$ | 5 | 85 |
| 65. | $V_4$ $V_{15}$ $V_{25}$ $V_{32}$ $V_{35}$ | 5 | 69 |
| 66. | $V_4$ $V_{15}$ $V_{25}$ $V_{33}$ $V_{35}$ | 5 | 67 |
| 67. | $V_6$ $V_{15}$ $V_{25}$ $V_{31}$ $V_{35}$ | 5 | 94* |
| 68. | $V_6$ $V_{15}$ $V_{25}$ $V_{32}$ $V_{35}$ | 5 | 87 |
| 69. | $V_6$ $V_{15}$ $V_{25}$ $V_{33}$ $V_{35}$ | 5 | 82 |
| 70. | $V_9$ $V_{15}$ $V_{25}$ $V_{31}$ $V_{35}$ | 5 | 95* |
| 71. | $V_9$ $V_{15}$ $V_{25}$ $V_{32}$ $V_{35}$ | 5 | 88 |
| 72. | $V_9$ $V_{15}$ $V_{25}$ $V_{33}$ $V_{35}$ | 5 | 83 |
| 73. | $V_{13}$ $V_{15}$ $V_{25}$ $V_{31}$ $V_{35}$ | 5 | 85 |
| 74. | $V_{13}$ $V_{15}$ $V_{25}$ $V_{32}$ $V_{35}$ | 5 | 60 |
| 75. | $V_{13}$ $V_{15}$ $V_{25}$ $V_{33}$ $V_{35}$ | 5 | 60 |
| 76. | $V_2$ $V_{15}$ $V_{17}$ $V_{22}$ $V_{31}$ $V_{35}$ $V_{36}$ | 7 | 51 |
| 77. | $V_3$ $V_{15}$ $V_{17}$ $V_{22}$ $V_{31}$ $V_{35}$ $V_{36}$ | 7 | 50 |
| 78. | $V_4$ $V_{15}$ $V_{17}$ $V_{22}$ $V_{31}$ $V_{35}$ $V_{36}$ | 7 | 54 |
| 79. | $V_2$ $V_{15}$ $V_{22}$ $V_{24}$ $V_{31}$ $V_{35}$ $V_{36}$ | 7 | 50 |
| 80. | $V_3$ $V_{15}$ $V_{22}$ $V_{24}$ $V_{31}$ $V_{35}$ $V_{36}$ | 7 | 51 |
| 81. | $V_4$ $V_{15}$ $V_{22}$ $V_{24}$ $V_{31}$ $V_{35}$ $V_{36}$ | 7 | 52 |
| 82. | $V_2$ $V_{15}$ $V_{17}$ $V_{27}$ $V_{31}$ $V_{36}$ | 6 | 58 |
| 83. | $V_3$ $V_{15}$ $V_{17}$ $V_{22}$ $V_{31}$ $V_{36}$ | 6 | 54 |
| 84. | $V_4$ $V_{15}$ $V_{17}$ $V_{22}$ $V_{31}$ $V_{36}$ | 6 | 60 |
| 85. | $V_2$ $V_{15}$ $V_{22}$ $V_{24}$ $V_{31}$ $V_{36}$ | 6 | 52 |
| 86. | $V_3$ $V_{15}$ $V_{22}$ $V_{24}$ $V_{31}$ $V_{36}$ | 6 | 55 |

TABLE 4-5 (*Contd.*)

| S. No. | Variables | Number of Variables | Percentage Correctly Classified |
|---|---|---|---|
| 87. | $V_4$ $V_{15}$ $V_{22}$ $V_{24}$ $V_{31}$ $V_{36}$ | 6 | 54 |
| 88. | $V_2$ $V_{12}$ $V_{15}$ $V_{22}$ $V_{24}$ $V_{31}$ $V_{35}$ $V_{36}$ | 8 | 56 |
| 89. | $V_4$ $V_{12}$ $V_{15}$ $V_{22}$ $V_{24}$ $V_{31}$ $V_{35}$ $V_{36}$ | 8 | 49 |
| 90. | $V_9$ $V_{25}$ $V_{35}$ | 3 | 91 |
| 91. | $V_6$ $V_{31}$ $V_{35}$ | 3 | 90 |
| 92. | $V_2$ $V_{31}$ $V_{35}$ | 3 | 87 |
| 93. | $V_9$ $V_{31}$ $V_{35}$ | 3 | 92 |
| 94. | $V_2$ $V_{35}$ | 2 | 80 |
| 95. | $V_2$ $T_{31}$ | 2 | 90 |
| 96. | $V_9$ $V_{31}$ | 2 | 90 |
| 97. | $V_9$ $V_{35}$ | 2 | 87 |
| 98. | $V_6$ $V_{31}$ | 2 | 77 |
| 99. | $V_6$ $V_{35}$ | 2 | 80 |

*Note*: The predicted results marked with * are selected for further analysis.

After screening the predictive accuracy of various discriminant functions shown in Table 4-5, seven sets of variables predicting the company failure accurately 93 per cent and above one year prior to the event i.e. failure were chosen for further analysis. The seven ratio-profiles and their predictive results are shown in Table 4-6.

To arrive at the final profile of variables doing the best overall job together in the prediction of company failure, seventeen new combinations of variables shown in Table 4-6 were formulated and the predictive accuracy of each profile for each of the year before failure (i.e. six years) was ascertained by the use of discriminant analysis. The discriminant functions and the predicted results of each function for the period of one to six years prior to failure are shown in Table 4-7.

TABLE 4-6. **Predictive Accuracy of Seven Discriminant Functions One Year Prior to Failure**

| S. No. | Variables | Number of Variables | Percentage Correctly Classified |
|---|---|---|---|
| 10. | $V_9$ $V_{15}$ $V_{16}$ $V_{31}$ $V_{35}$ | 5 | 94 |
| 25. | $V_9$ $V_{15}$ $V_{17}$ $V_{31}$ $V_{35}$ | 5 | 93 |
| 40. | $V_9$ $V_{15}$ $V_{23}$ $V_{31}$ $V_{35}$ | 5 | 93 |
| 55. | $V_9$ $V_{15}$ $V_{24}$ $V_{31}$ $V_{35}$ | 5 | 93 |
| 61. | $V_2$ $V_{15}$ $V_{25}$ $V_{31}$ $V_{35}$ | 5 | 94 |
| 67. | $V_6$ $V_{15}$ $V_{25}$ $V_{31}$ $V_{35}$ | 5 | 94 |
| 70. | $V_9$ $V_{15}$ $V_{25}$ $V_{31}$ $V_{35}$ | 5 | 95 |

Any function which satisfies the two conditions given below was selected as the final best discriminant function:

(1) the discriminant function which results in the least percentage classification error over a period of one to six years prior to the date of failure; and
(2) the least percentage of misclassification at the earliest possible time (6th year in this study) before company failure.

From the Table 4-7, it is clear that the discriminant function-4 satisfies the above mentioned two conditions for selecting the best profile of ratios in predicting company failure. The discriminant function-4 results in the least percentage error rates in classification of companies in the sample either in one of the group over a period of six years prior to failure and also the least percentage of classification error in the 6th year prior to failure. Though the predictive accuracy of discriminant functions-1, 2, 3, 5, 6, 7, 11 in Table 4-7 one year prior to failure is equivalent to the predicted results of discriminant function-4 (i.e. 95%), but it falls rapidly compared to discriminant function-4 as the lead period before the company failure increases. The predicted results of

TABLE 4-7. **Predictive Accuracy of Seventeen Discriminant Functions for the Period of Six Years Prior to Failure**

(*In percentages*)

| Discriminant Function | Cut off Point | Year Prior to Failure | | | | | |
|---|---|---|---|---|---|---|---|
| | | 1st | 2nd | 3rd | 4th | 5th | 6th |
| 1. $Y=17.0684V_2-.5872V_{17}+.7802V_{35}$ | 0.501 | 95 | 81 | 82 | 68 | 62 | 73 |
| 2. $Y=20.3118V_9+.0073V_{25}+.6586V_{31}$ | 1.0604 | 95 | 85 | 84 | 82 | 78 | 75 |
| 3. $Y=22.0264V_9-.6613V_{16}+.8178V_{31}+.9530V_{35}$ | 0.7515 | 95 | 83 | 84 | 80 | 73 | 75 |
| 4. $Y=19.8927V_9+.0047V_{25}+.7141V_{31}+.4860V_{35}$ | 1.425 | 95 | 87 | 86 | 82 | 79 | 78 |
| 5. $Y=19.4533V_9+.0931V_{15}+.8120V_{31}+.5532V_{35}$ | 1.750 | 95 | 70 | 71 | 65 | 68 | 61 |
| 6. $Y=14.0754V_2+.0902V_{15}+.9626V_{31}+.8499V_{35}$ | 2.200 | 95 | 86 | 83 | 69 | 68 | 73 |
| 7. $Y=10.0671V_6+.0097V_{25}+.8622V_{31}+.7024V_{35}$ | 1.750 | 95 | 79 | 80 | 68 | 67 | 69 |
| 8. $Y=9.7910V_6+.0951V_{15}+.9555V_{31}+.7611V_{35}$ | 1.750 | 94 | 78 | 76 | 65 | 68 | 83 |
| 9. $Y=14.5166V_2+.0015V_{25}+.8715V_{31}+.7914V_{35}$ | 1.500 | 94 | 82 | 86 | 75 | 71 | 76 |
| 10. $Y=22.3105V_9-.0679V_{17}+.8075V_{31}+.9385V_{35}$ | 1.500 | 94 | 83 | 79 | 80 | 75 | 76 |
| 11. $Y=19.5975V_9+.0939V_{15}+.0112V_{25}+.8085V_{31}+.5455V_{35}$ | 1.803 | 95 | 85 | 84 | 80 | 76 | 75 |

| | | | | | | | |
|---|---|---|---|---|---|---|---|
| 12. $Y = 14.1613V_2 + .0907V_{15} + .0073V_{25} + .9610V_{31} + .8462V_{35}$ | 1.960 | 94 | 87 | 84 | 67 | 70 | 76 |
| 13. $Y = 9.7554V_6 + .0949V_{15} + .0035V_{25} + .9563V_{31} + .7633V_{35}$ | 1.500 | 94 | 82 | 79 | 68 | 71 | 71 |
| 14. $Y = 21.7631V_9 + .1003V_{15} - .7044V_{16} + .9280V_{31} + .1.0518V_{35}$ | 0.800 | 94 | 83 | 80 | 78 | 70 | 71 |
| 15. $Y = 20.1804V_9 + .0909V_{15} - .5836V_{23} + .8843_{31} + .8788V_{35}$ | 1.350 | 93 | 83 | 80 | 78 | 70 | 71 |
| 16. $Y = 22.0508V_9 + .1007V_{15} - .7202V_{17} + .9169V_{31} + .1.0344V_{35}$ | 1.300 | 93 | 82 | 79 | 78 | 68 | 75 |
| 17. $Y = 20.5628V_9 + .0976V_{15} + .4058V_{24} + .8658V_{31} + .9180V_{35}$ | 1.730 | 93 | 86 | 83 | 78 | 75 | 75 |

discriminant function-4 over a period of six years prior to failure are more consistent and better as compared to the predictive accuracy of all other discriminant functions shown in Table 4-7. Thus, the discriminant function-4 has been chosen as the best profile of ratios in predicting the chances of survival or failure of a company. The discriminant model so developed is not claimed to be optimal, since the process is iterative, it, however, does the best job among the alternatives which include numerous computer runs and analysis of various ratio-profiles. The final best discriminant function is as under:

$$Y = 19.8927V_9 + 0.0047V_{25} + 0.7141V_{31} + 0.4860V_{35}$$

where

$Y$ = Overall discriminant score

$V_9$ = Earning before Interest and Taxes/Total Tangible Assets

$V_{25}$ = Current Assets/Current Liabilities

$V_{31}$ = Net Sales/Total Tangible Assets

$V_{35}$ = Defensive Assets/Total Operating Expenditures.

The variables in the above discriminant function are independent and least correlated with each other in both the groups, namely, failed group and non-failed group and thus each variable provides additional information about the financial health of a company. The contribution of each variable is additional towards the predictive power of the discriminant function. The correlation matrix given in Table 4-8 indicates the inter-correlations between the variables in the discriminant model.

$V_9$—*Earning Before Interest and Taxes/Total Tangible Assets*

This ratio is a measure of the true productivity of the company's assets, abstracting from any tax or leverage factors. It is expressed as:

$$\frac{\text{Earning Before Interest and Taxes}}{\text{Total Tangible Assets}}$$

It indicates how effectively the operating assets are being employed in generating profits. The ratio attempts to reflect

TABLE 4-8. **Correlation Matrix of Variables in the Discriminant Model**

| | $V_9$ | $V_{25}$ | $V_{31}$ | $V_{35}$ |
|---|---|---|---|---|
| $V_9$ | 1.00 | .189<br>(.174) | —.208<br>(.391) | .095<br>(—.165) |
| $V_{25}$ | .189<br>(.174) | 1.00 | —.176<br>(.443) | —.016<br>(.196) |
| $V_{31}$ | —.208<br>(. 91) | —.176<br>(.443) | 1.00 | —.254<br>(—.421) |
| $V_{35}$ | .095<br>(—.165) | —.016<br>(.196) | —.254<br>(—.421) | 1.00 |

*Note*: Top row of numbers indicates the intercorrelations between variables of group-1; the bottom row of numbers, enclosed in parantheses, represents the intercorrelations between variables of group-2.

all the consequences of operations of the company as well as the external events that might have affected it. This is a real test of economic success or failure of the firm [100]. Since the survival of a company is based on the earning power of its assets, this ratio appears to be appropriate particularly for the studies dealing with the prediction of chances of survival or failure of a company. A smaller EBIT/TTA ratio of a company is claimed to provide premonition of financial crisis in the future. Therefore, a negative relationship is understood to exist between this ratio and the probability of company's failure.

$V_{25}$—*Current Assets/Current Liabilities (CA/CL)*

This measure is defined as the ratio of current assets to current liabilities:

$$\text{Current ratio} = \frac{\text{Current Assets}}{\text{Current Liabilities}}$$

Current assets include cash and those assets which are converted into cash within a year, such as marketable securities, debtors and inventories. All obligations maturing within a year are included in current liabilities. Thus, current liabilities include creditors, bills payable, accrued expenses, bank overdraft, income tax liability. It indicates the availability of current assets in rupees for every one rupee of current liability. Current ratio provides an idea about the cushion available with the firm to meet its short-term liabilities. It represents a margin of safety for short-term creditors. If an enterprise cannot meet its short-term obligations as they become due, its continued existence becomes doubtful and that renders all other measures of performance irrelevant. Therefore, the liquidity crisis generally leads to solvency crisis. Current ratio, therefore, aids in the prediction of future company failure. Since current assets are generally regarded as the reservoir from which maturing obligations can be paid, it seems reasonable to assume that larger the current ratio, smaller the probability of failure.

$V_{31}$—*Net Sales/Total Tangible Assets*

This ratio is calculated by dividing net sales by total tangible assets of the firm

$$\text{Total Tangible Assets Turnover Ratio} = \frac{\text{Net Sales}}{\text{Total Tangible Assets}}$$

The total assets turnover ratio is a significant ratio since it shows the company's ability of generating sales from all the financial resources committed to the firm. As this ratio increases, there is more revenue generated per rupee of total investment in assets. A higher ratio of net sales/total tangible assets gives an indication of a higher degree of efficiency in the utilisation of assets. Higher the ratio, more efficient the utilisation of resources and, therefore, the smaller the probability of financial problems. The higher turnover brings forth fair return and even if the profit margin is small, the total return on investment shall be large enough to overcome any financial difficulties. Therefore, a lower turnover of total assets is generally treated as a precursor of financial crisis and thus, an indicator of corporate sickness.

$V_{35}$—*Defensive Assets/Total Operating Expenditures*

This measure indicates the defensive position of the firm

[101,102]. This calculates the interval of time for which the company can finance its continuing operations (without acquiring additional assets or paying down liabilities) from its liquid assets without resorting to cash flows from sales or from other short-term sources of finance. This ratio, known as 'Defensive interval ratio', is calculated by dividing the defensive assets by daily operating expenditures of the firm. In this study, it is calculated by dividing the defensive assets by total operating expenditures in order to determine it in terms of times instead of days. Defensive assets or quick assets include cash, marketable securities and receivables; the denominator of the ratio consists of operating expenses minus depreciation, depletion and amortization. Depreciation, depletion and amortization are excluded from operating expenses, because they are not current drain on cash and its equivalent. This ratio is relatively new to the accounting literature. It indicates the liquidity position of a firm more clearly. A smaller ratio of a firm indicates that the firm can operate on existing liquid assets for a shorter period as compared to the firm having high ratio, if all other sources of short term finance are cut off. Therefore, a smaller defensive interval ratio is considered a sign of liquidity crisis and thus, an indicator of company failure. A negative relationship is understood to exist between this ratio and corporate failure.

The coefficients of discriminant function and the cut off point which tends to minimise errors of classification of failed companies and non-failed companies are worked out as under:

To begin with, it is assumed that some unknown set of weighting coefficients exist which would define a composite score providing maximum discrimination between the two groups, namely, failed group of companies and non-failed group of companies. The simplest form which the desired discriminant function can take is the linear one :

$$Y=\lambda_1 V_1+\lambda_2 V_2+\lambda_3 V_3+\ldots+\lambda_n V_n$$

where Y is the composite score or index that is desired, $V_1, V_2, V_3, \ldots, V_n$ are the variables measured and $\lambda_1$, $\lambda_2$, $\lambda_3, \ldots \lambda_n$ (lambedas) are the corresponding weighting coefficients. The immediate task is to determine optimal values for the weighting coefficients $(\lambda_1, \lambda_2, \lambda_3, \ldots \lambda_n)$ such that the difference between mean scores for the two groups is maximised relative to the variation within groups. The optimum weighting coefficients providing maximum discrimination between the two groups, namely, failed group and non-failed group are obtained by multiplying the inverse of the within groups variance-covariance matrix by the vector of mean differences. It can be presented in a matrix notation form:

$$=c^{-1}d$$

where $c^{-1}$ is the inverse of the within-groups variance-covariance matrix, d is the vector of mean differences; and $\lambda$ represents the weighting coefficients defining the best discriminating linear combination of the original $V_n$ scores. The mean values of the four finally selected variables (i.e. financial ratios) of both the groups; the difference between the mean values; and the inverse of the within groups variance-covariance matrix are shown below in Table 4-9.

TABLE 4-9A. **Means of Original Variables Selected for the Discriminant Model**

| Variables | GR-1 | GR-2 | (d) |
|---|---|---|---|
| $V_9$-EBIT/TTA | --0.09389 | 0.11989 | 0.21378 |
| $V_{25}$-CA/CL | 1.44268 | 3.39694 | 1.95426 |
| $V_{31}$-NS/TTA | 0.61282 | 1.85912 | 1.24630 |
| $V_{35}$-DA/TOE | 0.28210 | 0.48379 | 0.20169 |

*Notes*: GR-1: represents failed firms
GR-2: represents non-failed firms
d: denotes the vector of mean differences.

TABLE 4-9B. **Within Groups Variance-Covariance Inverse Matrix of Variables in the Discriminant Model**

| Variables | $V_9$ | $V_{25}$ | $V_{31}$ | $V_{35}$ |
|---|---|---|---|---|
| $V_9$ | 104.21127 | --0.27278 | —1.08841 | —2.46642 |
| $V_{25}$ | —0.27278 | 0.02560 | 0.00802 | 0.01509 |
| $V_{31}$ | —1.08841 | 0.00802 | 0.69423 | 0.32648 |
| $V_{35}$ | —2.46642 | 0.01509 | 0.32648 | 2.86029 |

From the row-by-column rule matrix multiplication, this is equivalent to setting each unknown $\lambda_i$ equal to a weighted sum of the elements in one row of the inverse matrix, each being weighted by the appropriate mean difference:

$$\lambda_i = d_1 c^{i1} + d_2 c^{i2} + d_3 c^{i3} + \ldots + d_J c^{iJ}$$

where $c^{iJ}$ is the element in the *i*th row and *j*th column of the inverse matrix and $d_J$ is the difference between mean values for the two groups on Jth variables. This multiplication results in the following equations:

$$\lambda_9 = .21378\ (104.21127) + 1.95426\ (-.27278) + 1.24630\ (-1.08841) + .20169\ (-2.46642)$$

$$\lambda_{25} = .21378\ (-.27278) + 1.95426\ (.02560) + 1.24630\ (.00802) + .20169\ (.01509)$$

$$\lambda_{31} = .21378(-1.08841) + 1.95426(.00802) + 1.24630(.69423) + .20169(.32648)$$

$$\lambda_{35} = .21378(-2.46642) + 1.95426(.01509) + 1.24630(.32648) + .20169(2.86029).$$

Solution of these equations yields the following values of discriminant coefficients

$$\lambda_9 = +19.8927$$
$$\lambda_{25} = +0.0047$$
$$\lambda_{31} = +0.7141$$
$$\lambda_{35} = +0.4860.$$

To test the statistical significance of overall discriminating power of the discriminant function (i.e. $Y = 19.8927V_9 + 0.0047V_{25} + 0.7141V_{31} + 0.4860V_{35}$), multivariate F-ratio was worked out. F-value is the ratio of the sums of squares (i.e. variances) between groups to the sums of squares (within-groups. If this ratio is maximised, it has the effect of separating the means of the two groups and similarly reducing the dispersion of the individual points about their group means.

Symbolically:

$$F = \frac{(\bar{Y}_{g1} - \bar{Y}_{g2})^2}{\sum_{i=1}^{ng_1} (Y_i - \bar{Y}_{g1})^2 + \sum_{i=1}^{ng_2} (Y_i - \bar{Y}_{g2})^2}$$

where

$(Y_{g1}-Y_{g2})^2$=Sum of variance between the groups means

$(Y_i-Y_{g1})^2+(Y_i-Y_{g2})^2$=Sum of variances within groups

$g$=Number of groups

$ng$=Number of observations in group $g$

$Y_i$=Score of individual observation

Y=Group mean.

Mean discriminant function values i.e. $Y_{g1}$ and $Y_{g2}$ of the failed group and non-failed group are computed by applying the weighting coefficients to the group means of the original variables (i.e. $V_9$, $V_{25}$, $V_{31}$, $V_{35}$):

$$Y_{g1}=19.8927(-.09389)+.0047(1.44268)+.7141(.61281)+.4860(.28210)$$

$$Y_{g2}=19.8927(.11989)+.0047(3.39694)+.7141(1.85912)+.4860(.48379).$$

Solution of the above equations and F-ratio formula yields the following values:

$$Y_{g1}=-1.2862$$

$$Y_{g2}=3.9635$$

$$F=24.4976$$

$$F_{1,76}(.01)=6.98.$$

The values given above were worked out on IBM 360/44 computer available at Delhi University Computer Centre.

The significance test of the overall discriminating power of the discriminant function rejects the null hypothesis that the observations come from the same population. It is, therefore, concluded that *a priori* groups are significantly different from each other and it leaves no doubts as to the discriminating power of the discriminant function.

The relative contribution of each variable to the total discriminating power of the function is also determined on the basis of scaled vector of each variable which is computed by multiplying corresponding elements by the square roots of the diagonal elements of the variance-covariance matrix. The scaled vector for each variable (ratio) is worked out by taking the following steps:

(a) Square root of diagonal elements of each of the variable in the variance-covariance matrix is obtained; and
(b) discriminant coefficient of each of the variable is multiplied by the concerned square root of the diagonal element in the variance-covariance matrix.

Since the actual variable measurement units are not comparable to each other, simple observation of the discriminant coefficients may mislead. The adjusted coefficients (i.e. scaled vectors), therefore, are computed and presented in Table 4-10. These adjusted coefficients enable us to evaluate the relative contribution of each variable towards discriminant index.

TABLE 4-10. **Scaled Vectors indicating Relative Contribution of the Variables**

| Variable | Scaled Vector | Ranking |
|---|---|---|
| $V_9$-EBIT/TTA | 2.009 | 1 |
| $V_{25}$-CA/CL | 0.033 | 4 |
| $V_{31}$-NS/TTA | 0.885 | 2 |
| $V_{35}$-DA/TOE | 0.298 | 3 |

The scaled vectors presented in Table 4-10 clearly indicate that the profitability ratio (i.e. EBIT/TTA) contributes the most followed by the turnover ratio (i.e. NS/TTA) towards the discriminating power of the discriminant function and thus, rejects the null hypothesis.

Once the values of the discriminant co-efficients are determined, it is possible to calculate discriminant scores for each observation in the sample or any new firm and to assign the observation to one of the groups based on this score. The essence of the procedure is to compare the score of an individual firm with that of the alternative groups. In this manner, the firm is assigned to the group it most closely resembles.

Having selected the final best discriminant function, discriminant scores (Y-scores) of each of the individual observations are calculated one year prior to the event (i.e. failure) and presented below in Table 4-11.

TABLE 4.11 **Y-Score Values of 78 Companies in the Initial Sample One Year Prior to Failure**

| Co. Code Number | Y-Score (Discriminant Score) | Co. Code Number | Y-Score (Discriminant Score) |
|---|---|---|---|
| 101 | 0.322516 | 102 | —0.183123 |
| 103 | —7.479732 | 104 | 2.062744 |
| 105 | —1.625042 | 106 | —4.121619 |
| 107 | 0.695223 | 108 | 0.778460 |
| 109 | —0.124596 | 110 | —0.099117 |
| 111 | —1.092987 | 112 | 1.866842 |
| 113 | —2.998042 | 114 | —3.1394,8 |
| 115 | 0.363427 | 116 | 0.621903 |
| 117 | —0.076411 | 118 | —0.629480 |
| 119 | —0.306769 | 120 | —0.650435 |
| 121 | —3.019234 | 122 | 1.313031 |
| 123 | 3.367076 | 124 | 3.932187 |
| 125 | —0.012189 | 126 | —8.045675 |
| 127 | —0.789917 | 128 | —2.921009 |
| 129 | —1.018811 | 130 | —0.355697 |
| 131 | —3.111678 | 132 | —2.515463 |
| 133 | —4.084116 | 134 | —6.108268 |
| 135 | —1.275113 | 136 | —2.468291 |
| 137 | —2.816355 | 138 | —1.257897 |
| 139 | 0.148498 | 240 | 5.972725 |
| 241 | 5.835010 | 242 | 6.760247 |
| 243 | 1.804542 | 244 | 2.807704 |
| 245 | 2.246477 | 246 | 9.849155 |

| Co. Code Number | Y-Score (Discriminant Score) | Co. Code Number | Y-Score (Discriminant Score) |
|---|---|---|---|
| 247 | 4.040750 | 248 | 3.325727 |
| 249 | 3.880880 | 250 | 3.299144 |
| 251 | 3.168562 | 252 | 3.920242 |
| 253 | 2.363754 | 254 | 2.449077 |
| 255 | 3.491007 | 256 | 2.774686 |
| 257 | 3.763230 | 258 | 3.389658 |
| 259 | 4.316798 | 260 | 2.450748 |
| 261 | 3.067127 | 262 | 3.437861 |
| 263 | 4.336874 | 264 | 4.489725 |
| 265 | 3.267273 | 266 | 3.954998 |
| 267 | 4.852349 | 268 | 2.713541 |
| 269 | 3 587265 | 270 | 4.451972 |
| 271 | 4.658970 | 272 | 3.209098 |
| 273 | 3.910942 | 274 | 3.190253 |
| 275 | 1.705799 | 276 | 3.437982 |
| 277 | 2.130720 | 278 | 1.526115 |

*Notes*: First digit of the code number denotes the group; and next two digits denote the observations serial number in the sample.

### 4.2.2 *Determination of Cut off Point*

The discriminant model will have more practical applicability for investors, bankers, credit managers and executives if an attempt is made to extend the model for general application, which is possible only if a cut off point is selected for general applicability. Cut off point is an optimum value which results in minimum number of misclassification. The cut off point makes predictions possible without computer support which is not easily accessible for bankers, credit managers, executives and potential investors at all levels. A question, therefore, of more concern than mere statistical significance in most discriminant function analysis is the selection of a 'cut off' point and assignment of individuals to one of the two groups.

In this case, it is observed that each individual is certain to belong to one of the two groups, no other alternatives are available. If there is no basis for assuming that one group should contain substantially more observations than the other and if the seriousness of errors of misclassification is about equal, the logical 'cut off' point lies halfway between the two group means $\bar{Y}_{c_1}$ and $\bar{Y}_{g2}$ [88]:

$$Y_c = \frac{\bar{Y}_{g1} + \bar{Y}_{g2}}{2}$$

where

$Y_c$=Cut off point

$Y_{g1}$=Group-1 discriminant mean value

$Y_{g2}$=Group-2 discriminant mean value.

If the individual discriminant score is below $Y_c$, the individual should be classified in group-1 and if above $Y_c$, it should be assigned to group-2. It can be presented in an equation form by adding the constant—$Y_c$ to the discriminant function:

$$Y = -Y_c + \lambda_1 V_1 + \lambda_2 V_2 + \lambda_3 V_3 + \ldots + \lambda_n V_n$$

where $Y_c$=cut off point.

$V_1, V_2, V_3, \ldots, V_n$ are the variables measured and $\lambda_1, \lambda_2, \lambda_3, \ldots, \lambda_n$ are the corresponding weights.

The decision rule than becomes: assign to group-2 if the individual's discriminant score is positive and to group-1 if negative. This is known as a maximum likelihood procedure, because each individual is assigned to the group in which the occurrence of his particular discriminant score is most likely.

In this study, the discriminant cut off point (i.e. the value lying halfway between the two group means) is:

$$Y_c = \frac{Y_{g1} + Y_{g2}}{2}$$

$$Y_c = \frac{-1.2862 + 3.9635}{2} = 1.3386.$$

But an empirical method is adopted for determining the critical value to minimise total classification error rather than defining $Y_c$ arithmatically. Table 4-11 indicates that all companies having a *Y*-score greater than 3.9322 clearly fall into the non-failed group sector while those companies having a Y-score below 1.5261 are all failed companies. Thus, the area between 1.5261 and 3.9322 discriminant scores is defined as the 'Zone of Ignorance' because of susceptibility to error classification. Since errors are observed in this range of values, we will be uncertain about a new company whose Y-score falls within the 'Zone of Ignorance'. Hence, it is desirable to minimise this range of uncertainty and to establish a guideline for classifying companies falling in the 'Zone of Ignorance'.

The process begins by identifying companies which fall within the overlapping range. The companies falling within the 'Zone of Ignorance' are shown in Table 4-12.

Next, by starting with a $Y_c$ score towards the minimum and maximum score of the overlapping area, the range of *Y*-scores that results in the minimum number of misclassifications is determined. In the analysis, Y's between the indicated values produce the following misclassifications, shown in Table 4-13.

It is observed from Table 4-13 that the best critical value (i.e. cut off point) falls between 1.33—1.52 since this range of Y-scores results in minimum number of misclassifications. Therefore, 1.425, the mid point of the range $\left(\text{i.e. } \frac{1.33+1.52}{2}\right)$, is taken as the $Y_c$ value (i.e. cut off point) that discriminates best between the failed companies and non-failed companies. Of course, the real test of this 'optimum' $Y_c$ value lies in its discriminating power not only with the initial sample but also with the additional samples and population (companies) in general.

### 4.2.3 *Estimating Probabilities of Misclassification in Assignment of Individual Companies*

Probabilities of misclassification of cut off point (i.e. $Y_c$) and of each company is computed in order to judge the predictive accuracy of discriminant function more rigorously in the

TABLE 4.12. **Companies whose Y-Score Fall within the 'Zone of Ignorance'**

| Non-failed Co. Code No. | Y—Score ($Y_c$=1.33) | Failed Co. Code No. |
|---|---|---|
| 278 | 1.52 | |
| 275 | 1.70 | |
| 243 | 1.80 | |
| | 1.86 | 112 |
| | 2.06 | 104 |
| 277 | 2.13 | |
| 245 | 2.24 | |
| 253 | 2.36 | |
| 254 | 2.44 | |
| 260 | 2.45 | |
| 268 | 2.71 | |
| 256 | 2.77 | |
| 261 | 3.06 | |
| 274 | 3.19 | |
| 272 | 3.20 | |
| 265 | 3.26 | |
| 248 | 3.32 | |
| | 3.36 | 123 |
| 258 | 3.38 | |
| 262 | 3.43 | |
| 276 | 3.43 | |
| 255 | 3.49 | |
| 269 | 3.58 | |
| 257 | 3.76 | |
| 273 | 3.91 | |
| | 3.93 | 124 |

*Note:* The first digit of the co. code number represents its group with the last two digits locating the company within the group.

TABLE 4.13. **Number of Misclassifications using Y-score Criterions**

| Range of Y-Scores | Number Misclassified | Companies |
|---|---|---|
| 1.33—1.52 | 4 | 112, 104, 123, 124 |
| 1.52—1.70 | 5 | 278, 112, 104, 123, 124 |
| 1.70—1.80 | 6 | 278, 275, 112, 104, 123, 124 |
| 1.80—1.86 | 6 | 278, 275, 243, 104, 123, 124 |
| 1.86—2.06 | 6 | 243, 275, 278, 104, 123, 124 |
| 2.06—2.13 | 5 | 243, 275, 278, 123, 124 |
| 2.13—2.24 | 6 | 277, 243, 275, 278, 123, 124 |
| 2.24—2.36 | 7 | 245, 277, 243, 275, 278, 123, 124 |
| 2.36—2.44 | 8 | 253, 245, 277, 243, 275, 278, 123, 124 |
| 2.44—2.45 | 9 | 254, 253, 245, 277, 243, 275, 278, 123, 124 |
| 2.45—2.71 | 10 | 260, 254, 253, 245, 277, 243, 275, 278, 123, 124 |
| 2.71—2.77 | 11 | 268, 260, 254, 253, 245, 277, 243, 275, 278, 123, 124 |
| 2.77—3.06 | 12 | 256, 268, 260, 254, 253, 245, 277, 243, 275, 278, 123, 124 |
| 3.06—3.19 | 13 | 261, 256, 268, 260, 254, 253, 245, 277, 243, 275, 278, 123, 124 |
| 3.19—3.20 | 14 | 274, 261, 256, 268, 260, 254, 253, 245, 277, 243, 275, 278, 123, 124 |

TABLE 4-13 (*Contd.*)

| Range of Y-Scores | Number Misclassified | Companies |
|---|---|---|
| 3.20—3.26 | 15 | 272, 274, 261, 256, 268, 260, 254, 253, 245, 277, 243, 275, 278, 123, 124 |
| 3.26—3.32 | 16 | 265, 272, 274, 261, 256, 268, 260, 254, 253, 245, 277, 243, 275, 278, 123, 124 |
| 3.32—3.36 | 17 | 248, 265, 272, 274, 261, 256, 268, 260, 254, 253, 245, 277, 243, 275, 278, 123, 124 |
| 3.36—3.38 | 16 | 248, 265, 272, 274, 261, 256, 268, 260, 254, 253, 245, 277, 243, 275, 278, 124 |
| 3.38—3.43 | 17 | 258, 248, 265, 272, 274, 261, 256, 268, 260, 254, 253, 245, 277, 243, 275, 278, 124 |
| 3.43—3.49 | 19 | 262, 276, 258, 248, 272, 274, 265, 261, 256, 268, 260, 254, 253, 245, 277, 243, 275, 178, 124 |
| 3.49—3.58 | 20 | 255, 262, 276, 258, 248, 265, 272, 274, 261, 256, 268, 260, 254, 253, 245, 277, 243, 275, 278, 124 |
| 3.58—3.76 | 21 | 269, 255, 262, 276, 258, 248, 265, 272, 274, 261, 256, 268, 260, 254, 252, 245, 277, 143, 275, 278, 124 |

| Range of Y-Scores | Number Misclassified | Companies |
|---|---|---|
| 3.76—3.91 | 22 | 257, 269, 255, 262, 276, 258, 248, 265, 272, 274, 261, 256, 268, 260, 254, 253, 245, 277, 243, 275, 278, 124 |
| 3.91—3.93 | 23 | 273, 257, 269, 255, 262, 276, 258, 248, 265, 272, 274, 261, 256, 260, 254, 253, 245, 277, 268, 243, 275, 278, 124 |

problem of classification between failed companies and non-failed companies and to take the classification decision with more confidence. While it is important in the development of a discriminant function classification procedure to evaluate the long run probabilities of misclassification for all members of each group, it is recognized that such probabilities are not uniform for all possible discriminant scores. Individual firms whose discriminant scores lie near the best cut off point are more likely to be placed in the wrong group than those having extremely large or small discriminant scores. Therefore, it becomes a matter of importance to estimate the probability of misclassification of cut off point and of each company, which is obtained by computing the Z-scores of cut off point (i.e. $Y_c$) and discriminant scores of each company in the initial sample.

Z-scores of $Y_c$ are computed as follows:

$$Z_{g1} = \frac{Y_c - {}_1Y_g}{\sqrt{V(Y)}}$$

$$Z_{g2} = \frac{Y_c - Y_{g2}}{\sqrt{V(Y)}}$$

where

$Z_{g1}$=Standard Score deviation about the group-1 mean score

$Z_{g2}$=Standard score deviation about the group-2 mean score

$Y_c$=Cut off point

$\bar{Y}_{g1}$=Group-1 discriminant mean score

$\bar{Y}_{g2}$=Group-2 discriminant mean score

V(Y)=Within group variance of the discriminant scores.

In this study,

$Y_c = 1.425$

$\bar{Y}_{g1} = -1.2862$

$\bar{Y}_{g2} = 3.9635$

$V(Y) = 5.0540.$

Putting these values in the above formula of Z-scores:

$$Z_{g1} = \frac{1.425-(-1.2862)}{\sqrt{5.0540}}$$

$$Z_{g2} = \frac{1.425-3.9635}{\sqrt{5.0540}}$$

Solution of the above equations yields the following values:

$Z_{g1} = 1.21$

$Z_{g2} = 1.13.$

Having obtained the values of $Z_{g1}$ and $Z_{g2}$, the associated probability density values f ($Y_{g1}$) and f ($Y_{g2}$) as ordinates of the normal curve are taken from Table A. 1 (Areas and ordinates of the normal curve in terms of $x/\sigma$) [88, pp. 470-79].

The table values indicate that the probability of misclassification is $P_{g1}$=.1131 and $P_{g2}$=.1292 for failed companies and non-failed companies respectively, where $P_{g1}$ represents the prob ibility of misclassification for companies in group-1 and $P_{g2}$ represents the probability of misclassification' for companies in group-2. The term 'misclassification' in this context means that assignment of companies to failed or non-failed group on the basis of the best discriminant function is expected to disagree with the actual or *a priori* classification in 11.31 per cent and 12.92 per cent cases in group-1 and group-2 respectively. It confirms the predictive accuracy of the discriminant model and indicates that further investigation may be required only in 11.31 per cent firms in group-1 and 12.92 per cent firms in group-2 in order to classify them correctly.

The following steps are to be taken to calculate the probability of error of each company and its probability of belonging to each group:

(1) The discriminant scores of each company are transformed to *Z*-score deviations about the two group means. Symbolically:

$$Z_{g1i} = \frac{\bar{Y}_i - \bar{Y}_{g1}}{\sqrt{V(Y)}}$$

$$Z_{g2i} = \frac{Y_i - \bar{Y}_{g2i}}{\bar{Y}V(\bar{Y})}$$

where

$Z_{g1i}$ = *Z*-score deviation of ith company discriminant score about group-1 mean

$Z_{g2i}$ = *Z*-score deviation of ith company discriminant score about group-2 mean

$Y_i$ = discriminant score of ith company

$\bar{Y}_{g1}$ = group-1 mean discriminant score

$\bar{Y}_{g2}$ = group-2 mean discriminant score

V(Y) = within group variance of the discriminant scores.

2. The associated probability-density values of Z-score deviations of firms of each group are taken from the Table A-1. (Areas and ordinates of the normal curve in terms of $x/\sigma$) [88, pp. 470-79] and denoted by:

$f(Y_{g1i})$ = the probability-density value of ith company in group-1

$f(Y_{g2i})$ = the probability-density value of ith company in group-2.

The ratio of these ordinate values provide the required estimates of probability of the individual company's belonging to each group:

$$P_{g1i} = \frac{f(Y_{g1i})}{f(Y_{g1i}) + f(Y_{g2i})}$$

$$P_{g2i} = \frac{f(Y_{g2i})}{f(Y_{g1i}) + f(Y_{g2i})}$$

where

$P_{g1_i}$ = the probability of ith company's belonging to group-1

$P_{g2i}$ = the probability of ith company's belonging to group-2

For example, the probability of ith company's belonging to group-1 is estimated to be $P_{g1i} = .12$ and the probability of belonging to group-2 is estimated to be $P_{g2_i} = .88$.

Following the rule of assigning the ith company to the more probable group i.e. group-2 results in an estimated probability of error of $P_e = .12$ i.e. the probability that the ith company will be incorrectly classified is $P_e = .12$.

The probability of misclassification particularly of those companies whose discriminant scores fall within the zone of uncertainty (1.33—1.52) is to be evaluated before assigning them into either of the two groups, because the companies whose discriminant scores lie within the area of uncertainty are more likely to be placed in the wrong group than those falling beyond the area of uncertainty.

Unless the probability of individual firm's belonging to either of the two groups is clearly high, one should refrain from making a definite classification pending examination of additional information. Thus, the probability of individual firm's belonging to each group should be used as an additional aid alongwith the discriminant scores in predicting the chances of survival or failure, especially for those companies whose discriminant scores lie close to cut off point.

### 4.2.4 *Empirical Results*

Empirical results are presented in a format, called Membership Classification Chart or Accuracy Matrix. The classification for each sample is computed and presented in a matrix form:

**Membership Classification Matrix**
**or**
**Accuracy Matrix**

| Actual Group Membership | Predicted Group Membership | | |
|---|---|---|---|
| | GR-1 | GR-2 | Total |
| GR-1 | C | $M_1$ | — |
| GR-2 | $M_2$ | C | — |
| Total | — | -- | — |

The actual group membership is equivalent to the *priori* groupings and the model attempts to classify the given companies correctly. The nature of the model, which is explanatory at this stage, becomes predictive when new companies are classified.

In the Accuracy Matrix, C stands for correct classification and M stands for misclassification. On the basis of the accuracy matrix, percentage of correct classification and error rates are computed. $M_1$ represents a Type-I error and $M_2$, a Type-II error. The sum of diagonal elements equals the total correct (C) and when divided into the total number of companies classified (e.g. seventy eight in the case of initial sample), yields the measure of success of the Discriminant Model in classifying companies correctly. Accuracy of classification is the important factor in discriminant analysis [103]. Accuracy is considered in two dimensions:

Type-I, the accuracy of correctly classifying the failed companies and Type-II, accuracy of correctly classifying non-failed companies. Type-I error would be predicting a failed company not to fail, and a Type-II error would be predicting a non-failed company to fail. These two types of accuracy and error rates are presented in a format as under:

| | Number Correct | Total Number | %Correct | Number Incorrect | % Error |
|---|---|---|---|---|---|
| Type I | — | — | — | — | — |
| Type II | — | — | — | — | — |
| Total | — | — | — | — | — |

The two types of error usually do not produce equal penalty costs. For example, creditors might be more concerned to avoid Type-I because the magnitude of loss in capital may exceed expected return from interest payments. The cost of Type-II error is the opportunity cost of not lending to a debtor who would have been a good risk. In the anti-trust decision, a Type-II error might be more costly than Type-I. Allowing non-failed companies to go for complete merger because of predicting non-failed companies to fail, may do more harm to the interests of public than predicting failed companies not to fail. Therefore, the accuracy of the Discriminant Model is also to be assessed in the light of magnitude of Type-I and Type-II error.

## Accuracy of the Model

A series of tests are performed on the initial sample in order to judge the accuracy of the Discriminant Model in predicting company failure.

### 1. Predictive Accuracy One Year Prior to Failure

In this sample 39 companies in each of the two groups are examined using financial data one year prior to failure. In this case a high degree of successful classification is expected, because the discriminant function used for classification is derived from this sample. The predictive accuracy of the model for the initial sample is computed from Y-scores shown in Table 4-11 and presented in Table 4-14 in the form of a accuracy matrix.

It is observed from the Accuracy Matrix that the model proves to be very accurate in predicting the event. Its accuracy is 95 per cent in classifying the total sample into GR-1 and GR-2. The model is more accurate in classifying the non-failed companies (GR-2) where the accuracy is 100 per cent than GR-1 where the error rate is 10 per cent. It further strengthens the predictive power of the model. Though, the results are encouraging but the bias (sample and search bias) should not be overlooked. And therefore, further validation tests are to be conducted using the Discriminant Model to a

TABLE 4-14A. **Membership Classification or Accuracy Matrix One Year Prior to Failure**

| Actual Membership | | Predicted Membership | | |
|---|---|---|---|---|
| | | GR-1 | GR-2 | Total |
| GR-1 | | 35 | 04 | 39 |
| GR-2 | | 00 | 39 | 39 |
| | Total | 35 | 43 | 78 |

TABLE 4-14B

| | Number Correct | Total Number | % Correct | % Error |
|---|---|---|---|---|
| Type-I | 35 | 39 | 90 | 10 |
| Type-II | 39 | 39 | 100 | 00 |
| Total | 74 | 78 | 95 | 05 |

set of companies not used in the model building (discussed in Chapter V).

2. **Results Two Years Prior to Failure**

The second test is made to observe the discriminating ability of the model for companies using financial data two years prior to failure. With the help of discriminant model parameters, Y-scores of individual companies (seventy eight companies) are calculated and shown in Table 4-15.

Applying the cut off point ($Y_c$=1.425), determined on the basis of initial sample data one year prior to failure, the predictive accuracy of the model is calculated and presented in the accuracy matrix (Table 4-16).

TABLE 4-15. **Y-Score Values of Companies in the Initial Sample Two Years Prior to Failure**

| Co. Code Number | Y-Score | Co. Code Number | Y-Score |
|---|---|---|---|
| 101 | 0.2998 | 102 | 9.7321* |
| 103 | —9.0991 | 104 | 2.3244* |
| 105 | 0.2829 | 106 | 1.2907 |
| 107 | 0.9845 | 108 | 0.2504 |
| 109 | 0.0575 | 110 | —0.3760 |
| 111 | —8.8074 | 112 | 1.8263* |
| 113 | 1.5942* | 114 | 0.3819 |
| 115 | —7.0799 | 116 | —1.9465 |
| 117 | —4.5808 | 118 | 4.5493* |
| 119 | 0.0440 | 120 | —3.9136 |
| 121 | —3.0298 | 122 | 1.2812 |
| 123 | 4.5096* | 124 | 4.8189* |
| 125 | —0.1528 | 126 | —6.4537 |
| 127 | 1.0324 | 128 | —4.6645 |
| 129 | —1.2085 | 130 | —0.5413 |
| 131 | 3.2514* | 132 | 0.4417 |
| 133 | —1.9163 | 134 | —2.8810 |
| 135 | —2.2119 | 136 | 3.7099* |
| 137 | —1.6136 | 138 | —2.8984 |
| 139 | —1.3015 | 240 | 4.8104 |
| 241 | 7.5506 | 242 | 4.8959 |
| 243 | 8.1700 | 244 | 2.0655 |
| 245 | 1.9867 | 246 | 7.7861 |
| 247 | 1.9207 | 248 | 3.2972 |
| 249 | 2.8026 | 250 | 3.0606 |
| 251 | 3.3012 | 252 | 3.4007 |
| 253 | 2.7245 | 254 | 3.6447 |
| 255 | 6.7874 | 256 | 2.9462 |
| 257 | 1.4505 | 258 | 8.9810 |

| Co. Code Number | Y-Score | Co. Code Number | Y-Score |
|---|---|---|---|
| 259 | 7.1452 | 260 | 2.4824 |
| 261 | 3.8822 | 262 | 3.8865 |
| 263 | 4.4963 | 264 | 4.1428 |
| 265 | 1.7714 | 266 | 4.5922 |
| 267 | 4.3252 | 268 | 0.7029* |
| 269 | 1.7030 | 270 | 3.8879 |
| 271 | 3.5975 | 272 | 3.0974 |
| 273 | 3.9792 | 274 | 3.6765 |
| 275 | 1.5225 | 276 | 3.6309 |
| 277 | 6.7759 | 278 | 1.5609 |

*Note*: The misclassified companies are marked with*.

TABLE 4-16A. **Accuracy Matrix Two Years Prior to Failure**

| Actual Membership | Predicted Membership | | |
|---|---|---|---|
| | GR-1 | GR-2 | Total |
| GR-1 | 30 | 09 | 39 |
| GR-2 | 01 | 38 | 39 |
| Total | 31 | 47 | 78 |

TABLE 4-16B

| | Number Correct | Total Number | % Correct | % Error |
|---|---|---|---|---|
| Type-I | 30 | 39 | 77 | 23 |
| Type-II | 38 | 39 | 97 | 03 |
| Total | 68 | 78 | 87 | 13 |

Table 4-16 indicates that 30 companies out of 39 in group-1 and 38 companies out of 39 in Group-2 are correctly classified. This means that 68 companies out of 78 are correctly classified which amounts to 87 per cent predictive accuracy of the model two years prior to failure. The reduction in accuracy of the model in classifying the companies two years prior to failure is understandable and it was expected, because impending failure is more remote and the indications are less clear. Nevertheless, 87 per cent correct assignment of companies into respective groups is the evidence that failure/sickness can be predicted two years prior to the event (i.e. failure). Further tests are also performed to determine the long range predictive accuracy of the model in predicting company failure.

### 3. Long Range Predictive Accuracy of the Model

The predicted results of the model two years prior to the date of event (i.e. failure) are quite encouraging and justify its extension in the prediction of company failure beyond two years. Moreover, several studies (refer Chapter II) exhibited failure tendencies as much as five years prior to failure. Thus, an attempt has been made to ascertain the predictive accuracy of the model upto 6 years prior to failure. The data were collected for the 78 companies in the initial sample three to six years prior to failure. The reduced sample of firms in the above mentioned years prior to the event is on account of non-availability of financial statements for the more remote years. With the help of parameters of discriminant function, the Y-scores of individual companies are computed for each year before failure and presented below in Table 4-17.

TABLE 4.17. **Y-Score Values of Companies in the Initial Sample Three to Six Years Prior to Failure**

| Co. Code Number | Year Prior to Failure 3 | 4 | 5 | 6 |
|---|---|---|---|---|
| 101 | 0.6244 | —1.5799 | —2.7379 | —0.5654 |
| 102 | —0.8929 | —2.4083 | 1.2738 | 3.9452* |
| 103 | —2.3840 | —4.2674 | —1.3083 | —0.8348 |

TABLE 4-17 (*Contd.*)

| Co. Code Number | Year Prior to Failure | | | |
|---|---|---|---|---|
| | 3 | 4 | 5 | 6 |
| 104 | 3.1050* | 2.6699* | NA | NA |
| 105 | —0.8790 | —1.1065 | 0.2778 | NA |
| 106 | 0.3167 | 0.0162 | 1.8518* | 2.005* |
| 107 | 1.5223* | 0.7820 | NA | NA |
| 108 | —6.1263 | —0.9651 | —3.5874 | —2.5654 |
| 109 | NA | NA | NA | NA |
| 110 | —0.3850 | —0.5242 | NA | NA |
| 111 | —9.4767 | NA | NA | NA |
| 112 | 2.2666* | 2.9240* | 2.9590* | —0.3704 |
| 113 | 3.1905* | 4.4739* | 3.2997* | 3.1013* |
| 114 | 0.3150 | 2.1247* | 5.4462* | 2.5996* |
| 115 | —1.8240 | 0.4242 | 1.37[illegible]6 | 2.1038* |
| 116 | —2.7101 | —0.3170 | NA | —1.4245 |
| 117 | —8.8976 | —4.1930 | —3.1448 | —2.9714 |
| 118 | —0.3572 | 0.4805 | 3.6796* | 0.2787 |
| 119 | 0.2248 | 0.1123 | 0.5167 | NA |
| 120 | —0.3897 | —5.1537 | —2.1824 | —1.7318 |
| 121 | —3.5823 | —1.1611 | —1.4617 | —1.4556 |
| 122 | —1.8570 | —1.6874 | —0.6489 | —0.5094 |
| 123 | 0.7791 | —0.9227 | —0.1220 | NA |
| 124 | 2.7999* | 5.2811* | 5.4043* | 0.0617 |
| 125 | —0.7708 | 1.3148 | NA | NA |
| 126 | —7.9896 | —1.8373 | NA | NA |
| 127 | 0.7237 | —1.0895 | 1.2552 | 0.9166 |
| 128 | —1.8844 | 3.2009* | —0.1040 | —0.3171 |
| 129 | —0.8272 | —1.2325 | —0.6205 | 0.2411 |
| 130 | 0.8671 | —0.0297 | —5.3698 | NA |
| 131 | 2.5183* | —0.8381 | 0.3442 | 5.5352* |
| 132 | 1.7879* | 5.3232* | 4.0715* | 2.6589* |

| Co. Code | Year Prior to Failure | | | |
|---|---|---|---|---|
| Number | 3 | 4 | 5 | 6 |
| 133 | —3.3862 | NA | NA | NA |
| 134 | —1.0404 | —0.0132 | —2.5454 | 0.4298 |
| 135 | 1.3995 | 1.0149 | —0.1653 | 0.3261 |
| 136 | 4.0696* | 2.9525* | 2.0751* | 1.2560 |
| 137 | 0.4865 | 1.2167 | 1.1313 | 0.8379 |
| 138 | NA | NA | NA | NA |
| 139 | 0.5957 | 1.9430* | 1.8107* | 1.8192* |
| 240 | 4.6236 | 4.0383 | 3.1961 | NA |
| 241 | 4.5731 | 3.0026 | 3.6834 | 1.9083 |
| 242 | 5.6137 | 6.7232 | 5.6591 | NA |
| 243 | 2.9276 | —1.1196* | NA | NA |
| 244 | 2.5411 | 4.3074 | 2.3278 | 2.6856 |
| 245 | 1.8685 | 1.9450 | 1.6278 | 1.6992 |
| 246 | 5.1511 | 4.8190 | 3.0447 | 4.7289 |
| 247 | 1.5607 | 2.9489 | 3.8496 | 2.3477 |
| 248 | 3.8490 | NA | NA | NA |
| 249 | 4.5885 | 0.0072* | 4.1027 | 3.8495 |
| 250 | 0.6881* | 1.9708 | 2.2692 | 2.5363 |
| 251 | 0.1744* | 2.1101 | 2.7372 | NA |
| 252 | 3.2540 | 6.8127 | 5.5771 | 4.1122 |
| 253 | 2.9133 | 2.3401 | 2.5148 | NA |
| 254 | 2.2166 | 2.0927 | 1.7056 | 1.7962 |
| 255 | 3.9265 | 2.7302 | 1.8121 | 6.6372 |
| 256 | 2.0543 | —0.6369* | —1.4299* | 0.3505* |
| 257 | 2.5215 | 3.7921 | 2.5886 | NA |
| 258 | 3.9379 | 2.4517 | NA | NA |
| 259 | 6.1546 | 7.8454 | 8.7813 | 5.5526 |
| 260 | 2.1118 | NA | NA | NA |
| 261 | 4.7570 | 3.3488 | 4.1172 | NA |
| 262 | 2.8708 | 3.3042 | 2.3460 | 2.0771 |
| 263 | 5.6573 | 5.7375 | 6.0583 | 6.9574 |

TABLE 4.17 (*Contd.*)

| Co. Code Number | Year Prior to Failure 3 | 4 | 5 | 6 |
|---|---|---|---|---|
| 264 | 5.4862 | 3.6735 | —0.7089* | —2.7253* |
| 265 | 1.9586 | 1.4881 | 1.5617 | NA |
| 266 | 4.5550 | 2.3550 | 0.3666* | NA |
| 267 | 3.2412 | 4.2996 | 3.6741 | 3.6220 |
| 268 | 2.7629 | 3.0372 | 2.5568 | 1.7074 |
| 269 | 2.9196 | 3.3699 | 2.5558 | 1.1595* |
| 270 | 3.6141 | 3.3230 | 1.9780 | 2.7848 |
| 271 | 4.8721 | 3.8555 | 4.2476 | 3.1532 |
| 272 | 3.8620 | 5.3793 | 5.4078 | 4.9157 |
| 273 | 2.9133 | 1.5485 | 1.9124 | 2.5614 |
| 274 | 4.3529 | 4.4577 | 3.9732 | 5.3442 |
| 275 | 1.7193 | 3.1422 | 3.5615 | NA |
| 276 | 2.8503 | 2.2126 | NA | NA |
| 277 | 2.9827 | 4.3640 | 0.5591* | 2.0396 |
| 278 | 0.6890* | —0.2012* | 4.0578 | 4.5663 |

*Notes*: (1) The first digit of the co. code number denotes the group and the next two digits denote the serial number of the company.
(2) The misclassified firms are marked with*.
(3) Non-availability of data of a firm is denoted by NA.

The predictive accuracy of the model three to six years prior to failure is ascertained and presented in Table 4-18 in the form of a accuracy matrix.

From Table 4-18, it is evident that 65, 59, 50 and 40 companies are correctly classified out of 76, 72, 63 and 51 companies respectively in the sample three to six years prior to failure. It amounts to 86 per cent, 82 per cent, 79 per cent and 78 per cent predictive accuracy of the model three to six years prior to the event (i.e. failure) respectively. The reduction in the accuracy of the model is logically understandable

TABLE 4-18A. **Accuracy Matrix Three to Six Years Prior to Failure**

| Year Prior to Failure | Actual Membership | | Predicted Membership | |
|---|---|---|---|---|
| | | | GR-1 | GR-2 |
| 3 | GR-1 | 37 | 29 | 08 |
| | GR-2 | 39 | 03 | 36 |
| 4 | GR-1 | 35 | 26 | 09 |
| | GR-2 | 37 | 04 | 33 |
| 5 | GR-1 | 29 | 20 | 09 |
| | GR-2 | 34 | 04 | 30 |
| 6 | GR-1 | 26 | 18 | 08 |
| | GR-2 | 25 | 03 | 22 |

TABLE 4-18B

| Year Prior to Failure | Total Number of Firms | Number Correct | Per cent Correct | Per cent Error |
|---|---|---|---|---|
| 3 | 76 | 65 | 86 | 14 |
| 4 | 72 | 59 | 82 | 18 |
| 5 | 63 | 50 | 79 | 21 |
| 6 | 51 | 40 | 78 | 22 |

because as one goes back from the date of the event, the indicators (ratios) about the health of the unit become less and less clear.

## 4.3 Overall Performance of the Model

The predictive power of the model has been examined upto 6 years prior to the date of failure for initial sample and summarised in Table 4-19.

Table 4-19 clearly illustrates that it is possible to classify companies into either potentially failed or potentially non-failed groups upto six years prior to failure, though with decreasing probability. The fall in the accuracy of the model gradually increases as the lead time prior to the date of failure increases. The fall in accuracy of the model is logically understandable taking into account the long period that elapses because the indications of the ratios become less and less clear as the lead time from the date of the event increases. It is also clear from Table 4-19 that the model predicts well for the short

TABLE 4-19. **Summary of Six Years Predictive Accuracy of the Discriminant Model**

| Year Prior to Failure | Number of Companies | Number Correctly Classified | Number Misclassified | % of Correct Classification |
|---|---|---|---|---|
| 1 | 78 | 74 | 4 | 95 |
| 2 | 78 | 68 | 10 | 87 |
| 3 | 76 | 65 | 11 | 86 |
| 4 | 72 | 59 | 13 | 82 |
| 5 | 63 | 50 | 13 | 79 |
| 6 | 51 | 40 | 11 | 78 |

period as compared to the long period. If it is presumed that the period upto three years from the date of the event as a short period and from fourth year to sixth year as a long period, the fall in the accuracy of prediction is higher in the longer period than the short period, as shown in Table 4-20.

Table 4-20 clearly shows that the predictive accuracy of the model is higher in the short run than the long run. A higher degree of accuracy is available in the shorter period because the indications of failure from the study of the ratios are more clear in the short run than in the long run.

TABLE 4-20. **Comparison of Predictive Accuracy of the Model (Short Period and Long Period)**

| Year Prior to Failure | | % Accuracy of the Model | Fall in the Accuracy |
|---|---|---|---|
| Ist | Short Period | 95 | — |
| 2nd | | 87 | 8 |
| 3rd | | 86 | 9 |
| 4th | Long Period | 82 | 13 |
| 5th | | 79 | 16 |
| 6th | | 78 | 17 |

CHAPTER V

# Predictive Accuracy of the Model

## 5.0 Introduction

In this chapter, the model is applied to a new set of samples consisting of a cross-section of companies in order to judge its validity and effectiveness, since the efficiency of the model lies in predicting the chances of survival or failure of companies not used to develop the parameters of the model. Samples have also been drawn from a homogeneous group which means all companies in the group manufacture the same type of product. The chapter is presented under two sections. Section 5.1 deals with the applicability of the model to an industrial cross-section of companies. In Section 5.2, the model is empirically tested on a series of new samples of homogeneous group of companies.

## 5.1 Empirical Findings: Non-Homogeneous Group of Companies

*Sample of Failed Companies*

This sample consists of twenty four companies (Appendix M-1) taken irrespective of size, industry, age and fiscal year. In this case random sampling could not be followed on account of non-availability of data of failed companies. Availability of data, therefore, was the main criteria of including a company in the sample. Financial data of six years prior to failure were collected from the Library, Company Law Board, New Delhi and the discriminant tests were conducted using the data relating to the following years:

—Financial data for one year prior to the failure
—Financial data for two years prior to the failure

—Financial data for three years prior to the failure
—Financial data for four years prior to the failure
—Financial data for five years prior to the failure
—Financial data for six years prior to the failure

There is a reduction in the number of companies in the sample on account of non-availability of data, as the lead time prior to the event increases. The size of the sample for different years prior to failure is given below in Table 5-1.

TABLE 5-1 **The Number of Failed Companies on which Financial Data could be Obtained**

| Year Prior to Failure | Number of Companies |
|---|---|
| 1 | 24 |
| 2 | 24 |
| 3 | 21 |
| 4 | 15 |
| 5 | 15 |
| 6 | 14 |

Using the parameters established in the discriminant model i.e. $Y=19.8927V_9+0.0047V_{25}+0.7141_{31}+0.4860V_{35}$ (refer Chapter IV, pp. 88-89), the discriminant scores (Y-score values) are computed for each of the company for each year prior to failure and presented in Table 5-2.

On the basis of the cut off point ($Y_c=1.425$) as determined in the initial sample, the predictive accuracy of the model is ascertained and presented in Table 5-3.

Table 5-3 clearly indicates that out of 24 units in the sample, 23 units are classified correctly one year prior to the event. The discriminant model maintains 95.83 per cent accuracy in the classification of units one year prior to the failure. In case of two to six years prior to failure, the predictive accuracy of the discriminant model amounts to 95.83 per cent, 91.48 per cent, 93.75 per cent, 86 67 per cent and 86.67 per cent respectively. The predictive accuracy of the

TABLE 5-2 **Y-Score Values of Failed Companies in the Additional Sample of Non-Homogeneous Group One to Six Years Prior to Failure**

| Co. Code No. | Year Prior to Failure | | | | | |
|---|---|---|---|---|---|---|
| | 1 | 2 | 3 | 4 | 5 | 6 |
| F-01 | −12.6245 | −1.0141 | 0.3184 | −2.2773 | NA | NA |
| F-02 | 0.5364 | −1.3105 | −3.8558 | NA | NA | NA |
| F-03 | −1.0958 | −2.9167 | NA | NA | NA | NA |
| F-04 | −0.3345 | 0.9020 | −3.4637 | −2.3452 | 2.1567* | 0.4173 |
| F-05 | 1.0057 | −0.8221 | 1.0965 | 0.2213 | 0.0371 | 0.4954 |
| F-06 | −5.9403 | 1.3376 | 2.0031* | NA | NA | 2.0551* |
| F-07 | 0.6960 | 1.6830* | NA | NA | NA | NA |
| F-08 | −0.5686 | 0.7339 | 0.0665 | −2.8003 | 1.3957 | −0.1145 |
| F-09 | 1.0180 | 1.0423 | 0.6931 | 0.1991 | 0.5385 | 1.0519 |
| F-10 | 0.5537 | −3.2015 | −3.3602 | −0.8491 | 3.5479* | −2.3707 |
| F-11 | −2.1357 | 0.1668 | −3.0095 | 1.0929 | −3.5479 | −0.6477 |
| F-12 | −0.8505 | −1.4613 | −1.9525 | −1.9891 | −1.1075 | −0.6405 |
| F-13 | −0.2250 | −0.4535 | −0.1466 | −1.5752 | 1.1165 | −1.1166 |
| F-14 | −6.4120 | −6.9283 | −1.7723 | −0.6622 | −12.2285 | −4.7829 |
| F-15 | −16.5161 | −16.0449 | NA | NA | −8.5389 | −15.3251 |
| F-16 | −7.4280 | −5.6212 | −5.9058 | NA | NA | NA |

TABLE 5-2 (*Contd.*)

| Co. Code No. | Year Prior to Failure | | | | | |
|---|---|---|---|---|---|---|
| | 1 | 2 | 3 | 4 | 5 | 6 |
| F-17 | —0.5052 | 0.6920 | 0.1587 | NA | NA | NA |
| F-18 | 3.7326* | 0.5208 | 0.4785 | 0.8278 | 0.7916 | NA |
| F-19 | 0.6960 | 1.1112 | 0.6672 | NA | NA | NA |
| F-20 | —1.4614 | —3.9501 | −2.3711 | 0.4722 | —1.7349 | 0.9570 |
| F-21 | 0.9978 | —0.0315 | 4.0191* | 3.0132* | NA | NA |
| F-22 | —4.7567 | —1.4533 | 0.5282 | 0.5389 | —0.9148 | 1.0970 |
| F-23 | —0.9771 | —4.4510 | —0.7439 | 0.8126 | 0.3581 | 1.6710* |
| F-24 | 1.3685 | 0.5489 | —0.2651 | —2.5014 | —0.9568 | —0.2248 |

*Notes*: (i) F represents the failed unit and the digits 1-24 denote the serial number of firms in the sample.
(ii) The misclassified firms are marked with*
(iii) Non-Availability of data of a firm is denoted by (N.A.).

TABLE 5-3A **Accuracy Matrix of Failed Companies in the Additional Sample of Non-Homogeneous Group one to six years prior to failure**

| Year Prior to Failure | Actual Membership GR-1 | Predicted Membership GR-1 | Predicted Membership GR-2 |
|---|---|---|---|
| 1 | 24 | 23 | 01 |
| 2 | 24 | 23 | 01 |
| 3 | 21 | 19 | 02 |
| 4 | 16 | 15 | 01 |
| 5 | 15 | 13 | 02 |
| 6 | 15 | 13 | 02 |

TABLE 5-3B

| Year Prior to Failure | Type of Error | N | Number Correct | Percent Correct | Percent Error |
|---|---|---|---|---|---|
| 1 | Type-I | 24 | 23 | 95.83 | 04.17 |
| 2 | Type-I | 24 | 23 | 95.83 | 04.17 |
| 3 | Type-I | 21 | 19 | 90.48 | 09.52 |
| 4 | Type-I | 16 | 15 | 93.75 | 06.25 |
| 5 | Type-I | 15 | 13 | 86.67 | 13.33 |
| 6 | Type-I | 15 | 13 | 86.67 | 13.33 |

*Notes*: (i) Type-I represents Type-I error (refer Chap. III, p. 63)
(ii) N=Number of Observations in the sample
(iii) GR-1=Failed Group
(iv) GR-2=Non-Failed Group.

model is reduced to 86.66 per cent in the sixth year prior to failure from 95.83 per cent in one year prior to failure. It indicates that the accuracy of the discriminant model reduces as the lead period before failure increases. This is logically acceptable because as one goes back from the date of the event, the indicators (ratios) of the health of the unit become less and less clear.

A comparison of the predictive accuracy of the model for initial sample and the additional sample is made and presented below in Table 5-4.

TABLE 5-4. **Comparison of the Predictive Accuracy of the Model (Initial Sample and Additional Sample)**

| Year Prior to the Event | In Initial Sample % | In Additional Sample % |
|---|---|---|
| 1 | 95 | 95.83 |
| 2 | 87 | 95.83 |
| 3 | 86 | 90.48 |
| 4 | 82 | 93.75 |
| 5 | 79 | 86.67 |
| 6 | 78 | 86.67 |

It is clear from Table 5-4 that the predictive accuracy of the discriminant model is good, as in all additional samples the accuracy of the model is quite high in all the years prior to failure.

## 5.2 Empirical Findings: Homogeneous Group of Companies

In this section, the model is empirically tested with reference to homogeneous industry groups by taking a series of samples.

There is no doubt that the prediction of failure/sickness or survival of a firm can be done with greater confidence and reliability within a homogeneous industry group than across industry-groups on account of similarities in financial, technological and marketing characteristics. In order to test the effectiveness of the model in this area, an attempt has been made to collect data on homogeneous groups of companies and test applied.

### 5.2.1 *Additional Sample of Sick Textile Companies*

38 sick textile companies (Appendix M-2) were chosen from the list of sick cotton textile companies coming under the National Textile Corporation Limited. Availability of data (i.e. Financial statements) for the latest year before takeover of a firm was taken as the main criteria of including a firm in the sample for study. Financial data for a period of six years from the date of take over of a firm were collected from the Company Law Board Library, New Delhi and The Bombay Stock Exchange Directory.

The sample size is reduced due to non-availability of data as the period prior to take over of sick companies increases. The number of sick units for a period of six years before take over is shown below in Table 5-5.

TABLE 5-5 **The Number of Sick-Textile Companies on which Financial Statement Data could be Obtained**

| Year Prior to the Event (Take Over) | Number of Companies |
|---|---|
| 1 | 38 |
| 2 | 36 |
| 3 | 35 |
| 4 | 33 |
| 5 | 33 |
| 6 | 31 |

Using the discriminant model parameters i.e. $Y = 19.8927V_9 + 0.0047V_{25} + 0.7141V_{31} + 0.4860V_{35}$ (refer Chapter IV, pp. 88-89), the discriminant scores are calculated for each firm for a period of six years prior to take over and shown in Table 5-6.

On the basis of the cut off point ($Y_c = 1.425$), the accuracy matrix is prepared in order to ascertain the predictive accuracy of the model and presented in Table 5-7.

TABLE 5-6. **Y-Score Values of Sick-Textile Companies one to six years prior to Takeover**

| Co. Code No. | Year Prior to Take-Over/Failure 1 | 2 | 3 | 4 | 5 | 6 |
|---|---|---|---|---|---|---|
| ST-01 | 1.2166 | —6.8637 | —2.0467 | —0.3729 | —2.5474 | 0.6436 |
| ST-02 | —7.6316 | —1.9633 | —0.6038 | 1.3416 | 0.2008 | 0.9670 |
| ST-03 | 0.1803 | —2.1468 | —6.4561 | —2.6889 | —2.3429 | 0.9947 |
| ST-04 | 1.0959 | —0.1193 | —1.2450 | —2.0545 | 0.7369 | 1.3235 |
| ST-05 | 0.4470 | 0.3902 | 0.2628 | —0.5251 | 1.6287* | 2.3704* |
| ST-06 | 1.1824 | 0.6016 | —2.1739 | —9.8847 | —1.2972 | NA |
| ST-07 | —3.0095 | —6.5169 | —2.2430 | —1.4930 | NA | NA |
| ST-08 | —1.2783 | —0.3950 | 0.1658 | 1.7373* | 1.3460 | 2.1597* |
| ST-09 | —0.8945 | —3.2510 | —1.5399 | 0.9658 | 0.9500 | —3.5729 |
| ST 10 | 0.0618 | —1.6071 | 0.1028 | —1.1044 | 1.2657 | 2.1199* |
| ST-11 | —1.3410 | —3.6682 | —4.0519 | —4.8438 | 2.0001* | —3.1846 |
| ST-12 | 1.0434 | 1.2849 | —1.7376 | —7.7432 | —1.3229 | —2.1883 |
| ST-13 | —0.1128 | —0.5732 | —0.1374 | 1.2422 | 0.2935 | —0.8559 |
| ST-14 | —5.0412 | —0.8338 | —0.9388 | —1.0388 | 2.2331* | 2.0723* |
| ST-15 | —0.4906 | —6.4633 | 0.0780 | —0.8154 | 0.6778 | 0.4975 |

| | | | | | | |
|---|---|---|---|---|---|---|
| ST-16 | —3.2008 | —19.8089 | —0.3989 | —2.8612 | —2.2191 | 0.8825 |
| ST-17 | 0.8464 | —0.4674 | —0.4594 | —1.2216 | 1.1535 | —0.9123 |
| ST-18 | —0.7255 | —0.3938 | 0.2828 | 0.8508 | 0.6381 | —0.8301 |
| ST-19 | 0.2671 | 0.6280 | 0.5205 | NA | NA | NA |
| ST-20 | 0.3325 | —1.8967 | 0.9308 | —0.2656 | —2.6646 | NA |
| ST-21 | —2.4570 | 0.6358 | 0.5907 | 0.6357 | —0.2851 | —0.6337 |
| ST-22 | —1.1527 | —2.6968 | —1.7032 | —0.4417 | 0.4992 | —0.1690 |
| ST-23 | —1.6844 | 0.5228 | —0.8196 | —2.8837 | 1.1727 | 0.9703 |
| ST-24 | 0.9611 | —0.2294 | 0.0709 | —0.9072 | 0.7078 | 0.3532 |
| ST-25 | 0.2704 | 0.0510 | —2.2755 | —0.7777 | —1.6217 | 1.0073 |
| ST-26 | —1.3805 | —0.4260 | —12.6780 | 1.1916 | —1.0636 | 1.3412 |
| ST-27 | —2.0109 | 0.3556 | 0.3839 | NA | NA | NA |
| ST-28 | —0.1143 | —0.3615 | —0.9477 | 0.4131 | 1.2071 | 0.3427 |
| ST-29 | —4.0726 | —2.5933 | —2.0907 | —1.1872 | —1.5634 | —1.0396 |
| ST-30 | —2.0447 | —1.5483 | —1.5459 | —1.1468 | 1.0835 | 0.9656 |
| ST-31 | —4.2002 | —2.4259 | —0.8758 | 0.3582 | 1.3983 | 1.3535 |
| ST-32 | —4.3839 | —2.2403 | 0.2369 | —3.5289 | 0.2109 | 1.3075 |
| ST-33 | 0.4904 | 3.1340* | 3.6222* | 2.7632* | 0.8852 | 0.0285 |

TABLE 5·6 (*Contd*)

| Co. Code No. | Year Prior to Take-over/Failure | | | | | |
|---|---|---|---|---|---|---|
| | 1 | 2 | 3 | 4 | 5 | 6 |
| ST-34 | —0.2415 | NA | NA | NA | —0.3370 | —0.7038 |
| ST-35 | 0.0943 | 0.5132 | —0.9965 | —4.5785 | —8.6916 | —8.8215 |
| ST-36 | —2.1788 | 1.0576 | NA | 0.0311 | —1.3139 | —1.0530 |
| ST-37 | —0.7592 | —1.0610 | 1.2665 | NA | NA | NA |
| ST-38 | —2.9090 | NA | NA | NA | NA | NA |

*Notes*: (i) ST represents Sick Textile unit and the digits 1-38 denote the serial number of units in the sample.
(ii) The misclassified firms are marked with*
(iii) Non-availability of data of a firm is denoted by (N.A.).

TABLE 5-7A. **Accuracy Matrix of Sick Textile Companies One to Six Years Prior to the Event (i.e. Take Over)**

| Year Prior to the Event (Take Over) | Actual Membership GR—1 | Predicted Membership GR—1 | Predicted Membership GR—2 |
|---|---|---|---|
| 1 | 38 | 38 | 00 |
| 2 | 36 | 35 | 01 |
| 3 | 35 | 34 | 01 |
| 4 | 33 | 31 | 02 |
| 5 | 33 | 30 | 03 |
| 6 | 31 | 27 | 04 |

TABLE 5-7B.

| Year Prior to the Event (Take Over) | Type of Error | N | Number Correct | Percent Correct | Percent Error |
|---|---|---|---|---|---|
| 1 | Type-I | 38 | 38 | 99.00 | 00.01 |
| 2 | Type-I | 36 | 35 | 97.22 | 02.78 |
| 3 | Type-I | 35 | 34 | 97.14 | 02.86 |
| 4 | Type-I | 33 | 31 | 93.94 | 06.06 |
| 5 | Type-I | 33 | 30 | 90.91 | 09.09 |
| 6 | Type-I | 31 | 27 | 87.09 | 12.91 |

*Notes*: (i) Type-I represents type-I error (refer Chapter III, p. 63).
(ii) N=Total Number of Observations in the Sample
(iii) GR-1=Sick/Failed Group
(iv) GR-2=Non-Sick/Non-Failed Group.

The above Table 5-7 indicates that 38 units out of 38 in the sample are correctly classified which amounts to a very high degree of accuracy of the model in predicting sickness/failure of firms one year prior to failure. The percentage classification error rates are 0.0!,2.78,2.86, 6.06, 9.09 and 12.91 respectively one to six years prior to takeover/failure which shows that the model is very accurate in predicting the sickness of textile companies upto six years prior to take over. However, the performance of the model is relatively better in 1-3 years than 4-6 years prior to takeover/failure of firms.

The overall performance of the model in predicting sickness of textile companies is better compared to the predictive accuracy in the initial sample and the additional sample of failed companies which is clear from Table 5-8 presented below:

TABLE 5-8 **Percentage Classification Error in Predicting Failure/Sickness**

| Year Before Failure/ Sickness | In Non-Homogeneous Group | | In Homogeneous Group |
|---|---|---|---|
| | Initial Sample | Additional Sample of Failed Companies | Additional Sample of Sick Textile Companies |
| 1 | 05 | 04.17 | 00.01 |
| 2 | 13 | 04.17 | 02.78 |
| 3 | 14 | 09.52 | 02.86 |
| 4 | 18 | 06.25 | 06.06 |
| 5 | 21 | 13.33 | 09.09 |
| 6 | 22 | 13.33 | 12.91 |

The better results in case of homogeneous group of companies compared to the non-homogeneous group of companies must, in some measure, be due to the homogeneity of the industry group (cotton textiles) to which the model is applied.

5.2.2 *Additional Sample of Non-Failed Taxtile Companies*

35 non-failed textile companies (Appendix M-3) were selected at random irrespective of size and age from the list of companies

appearing in the Bombay Stock Exchange Directory. The financial data for a period of three years (1980, 1981, 1982) for each of the companywere collected. Three years period on continuous basis is considered sufficient for testing the chances of survival of a company or falling in the trap of sickness/failure. Using the parameters established in the discriminant model, the discriminant score values for each of the company for each year are computed and presented below in Table 5-9.

TABLE 5-9 **Y-Score Values of Non-Sick Textile Companies for the years 1980, 1981 and 1982**

| Co. Code No. | Years | | |
|---|---|---|---|
| | 1980 | 1981 | 1982 |
| NFT-01 | 5.4170 | 3.9846 | 3.8077 |
| NFT-02 | 2.7740 | 3.5647 | NA |
| NFT-03 | 4.3489 | 4.3558 | 3.6486 |
| NFT-04 | 3.2490 | 3.6131 | 2.8007 |
| NFT-05 | 5.0370 | 4.7085 | 1.2207*S |
| NFT-06 | 5.2144 | 3.1520 | 3.8212 |
| NFT-07 | 2.7843 | 3.0586 | 2.8744 |
| NFT-08 | 5.1766 | 4.3184 | 5.2483 |
| NFT-09 | 4.6305 | 4.2583 | 3.4791 |
| NFT-10 | 1.4598 | 4.5847 | 3.5847 |
| NFT-11 | 4.4044 | 4.0820 | 3.3739 |
| NFT-12 | 4.8026 | 3.9999 | 1.6414 |
| NFT-13 | 3.0273 | 3.4713 | 1.9054 |
| NFT-14 | 2.4732 | 2.1961 | 1.5338 |
| NFT-15 | 2.6304 | 2.1990 | 3.2422 |
| NFT-16 | 3.9454 | 3.5097 | 2.9315 |
| NFT-17 | 3.7706 | 3.2127 | 2.6276 |
| NFT-18 | 3.5641 | 1.8739 | 2.0292 |
| NFT-19 | 3.2725 | 2.7575 | 2.3860 |
| NFT-20 | 3.0288 | 2.2076 | 2.0517 |

TABLE 5-9 (*Contd.*)

| Co. Code No. | Years | | |
|---|---|---|---|
| | 1980 | 1981 | 1982 |
| NFT-21 | 4.7722 | 1.8551 | 4.5831 |
| NFT-22 | 4.1015 | 3.9731 | 5.0133 |
| NFT-23 | 3.8256 | 3.1876 | 0.4164*S |
| NFT-24 | 5.0060 | 4.6819 | 3.8656 |
| NFT-25 | 1.3395* | 1.7053 | 3.3043 |
| NFT-26 | 3.5409 | 4.5277 | 3.0238 |
| NFT-27 | 8.5108 | 6.9214 | 3.5093 |
| NFT-28 | 6.0771 | 3·2433 | 2.9382 |
| NFT-29 | 3.1599 | 2.8828 | 3.4812 |
| NFT-30 | 2.6304 | 1.4307 | 1.4229 |
| NFT-31 | 7.1608 | 6.0044 | 2.9833 |
| NFT-32 | 3.8537 | 1.7849 | 4.8707 |
| NFT-33 | 3.4387 | 3.3365 | 1.2642*S |
| NFT-34 | 6.4447 | 3.9059 | 1.6106 |
| NFT-35 | 3.1888 | 2.8175 | 3.0720 |

*Notes*: (1) NFT represents Non-failed Textile Companies and the digits 1-35 denote the serial number of firms in the sample.
(ii) The misclassified firms have been marked with*
(iii) S represents the workers' strike in the company.
(iv) The strike year is an abnormal year and thus, it is not included in the accuracy matrix.
(v) Non-availability of data of a firm is denoted by (N.A.).

Table 5-10 is derived from the above Table 5-9 and presented in the form of a accuracy matrix in order to determine the effectiveness of the model. The accuracy matrix or the membership classification matrix is prepared on the basis of the cut off point ($Y_c = 1.425$) established in the discriminant model to classify firms either in one of the groups—failed or non-failed group and presented below in Table 5-10.

TABLE 5-10A **Accuracy Matrix of Non-Sick Textile Companies for the years 1980, 1981 and 1982**

| Years | Actual Membership | Predicted Membership | |
|---|---|---|---|
| | GR-2 | GR-1 | GR-2 |
| 1980 | 35 | 01 | 34 |
| 1981 | 35 | 00 | 35 |
| 1982 | 31 | 00 | 31 |

TABLE 5-10B

| Years | Type of Error | N | Number Correct | Percent Correct | Percent Error |
|---|---|---|---|---|---|
| 1980 | Type-II | 35 | 34 | 97.14 | 02.86 |
| 1981 | Type-II | 35 | 35 | 100.00 | 00.00 |
| 1982 | Type-II | 31 | 31 | 100.00 | 00.00 |

*Notes*: (i) Type-II represents type II error (refer Chapter III, p. 63).
(ii) N=Total number of observations in the sample
(iii) GR-1=Failed/Sick Group
(iv) GR-2=Non-failed/Non-sick Group.

It is clear from Table 5-10 that the model amounts to a very high degree of accuracy in predicting the financial health of textile companies except the year 1980 in which 01 firm out of 35 is incorrectly classified. Though the predictive accuracy of the model is 97.14 per cent in 1980, but if we take the discriminant score of the misclassified firm (i.e. NFT-25 Y=1.3395), the accuracy of the model is somewhat higher than 97.14 per cent even in the year 1980. Because the

Y-score of the misclassified firm falls in the area of 'Zone of Ignorance' or 'temporarily sick firms' (i.e. between 1.33—1.52) which indicates that although the firm is classified as failed/ sick firm, the prediction is not as definite as the other firms getting the score beyond the 'Zone of Ignorance'. In such cases the probability of firm's belonging (refer Chapter IV, pp. 105-6) to each of the two groups-Failed/Sick and Non-failed/Non-sick group is to be calculated and the firm's position is to be examined on the basis of its Y-score and its probability of belonging to each group before it is classified into one of the two groups.

Another important observation is that the majority of the firms are getting lower discriminant score in the year 1982 compared to the year 1980 and 1981. The possible reasons are that the whole textile industry is affected by the severe recession in the market and to some extent by other abnormal factors such as strike of workers, power cut as mentioned in annual reports of some of the companies, for example, the companies with the following code no. NST-5, NST-23, NST-25, NST-33.

### 5.2.3 *Additional Sample of Non-failed Jute Companies*

19 non-failed jute companies (Appendix M·4) were selected on the basis of random sampling from the list of jute companies in the Bombay Stock Exchange Directory. In this case, the financial data for a period of four years (i.e. 1979, 1980, 1981 and 1982) were collected instead of three years, since there has been workers' strike in most of the companies in the sample in the year 1982. On the basis of the discriminant function i.e. $Y = 19.8927V_9 + .0047V_{25} + .7141V_{31} + .4860V_{35}$ (refer Chapter IV, pp. 88-89), the discriminant score values for each of the company for each year are computed and presented in Table 5-11.

Using the cut off point ($Y_c = 1.425$) the accuracy matrix is prepared and shown in Table 5-12.

The analysis of the results in Table 5-12 reveals that the model is very accurate in all the four years in predicting the financial health of jute companies. However, the probability of belonging (refer Chapter IV, pp. 105-6) to each group of

TABLE 5-11 **Y-Score Values of Non-Sick Jute Companies for the years 1979, 1980, 1981 and 1982**

| Co. Code No. | Years 1979 | 1980 | 1981 | 1982 |
|---|---|---|---|---|
| NFJ-01 | 2.0089 | 4.0483 | 3.9695 | 2.9080 |
| NFJ-02 | 4.1543 | 7.6389 | 2.2383 | 1.7712 |
| NFJ-03 | 6.2128 | 4.1265 | 2.8794 | 2.2510 |
| NFJ-04 | 4.1829 | 3.2142 | 2.1091 | 1.5398 |
| NFJ-05 | 4.0824 | 4.8326 | 2.5426 | 1.6459 |
| NFJ-06 | 2.2890 | 3.5876 | 2.3663 | 2.8064 |
| NFJ-07 | 1.4489 | 7.3955 | 1.9636 | —4.9008*S |
| NFJ-08 | 1.5029 | 3.7834 | 2.5101 | —0.9634*S |
| NFJ-09 | 3.6544 | 4.1147 | 2.6130 | 1.8840 |
| NFJ-10 | 4.5493 | 1.8344 | 5.8846 | NA |
| NFJ 11 | 3.3315 | 6.3583 | 5.8304 | 3.2108 |
| NFJ-12 | 2.2505 | 4.8456 | 2.7551 | 0.8818*S |
| NFJ- 3 | 1.4545 | 10.0752 | 2.4802 | —6.9594*S |
| NFJ-14 | 2.4029 | 7.9090 | 5.2257 | 2.3821 |
| NFJ-15 | 3.8352 | 6.1064 | 2.7615 | 0.7862*S |
| NFJ-16 | 1.5978 | 6.4501 | 2.0941 | —1.2523*S |
| NFJ-17 | NA | 5.3619 | 2.6620 | —0.7892*S |
| NFJ-18 | 2.0168 | 5.0986 | 3.4302 | 1.9038 |
| NFJ-19 | 4.7911 | 4.7411 | 2.6681 | —3.7348* |

*Notes*: (i) NFJ represents the non-failed jute unit and 1-19 represents the serial number of units in the sample.
(ii) The misclassified companies are marked with*
(iii) S denotes the strike in the company
(iv) The strike year is an abnormal year and therefore, it is not included in accuracy matrix for calculating the accuracy of the model.

firms' number NFJ-7, NFJ-8 and NFJ-13 in the year 1979 is to be calculated before taking any decision of membership

TABLE 5-12A **Accuracy Matrix of Non-Sick Jute Companies for the years 1979, 1980, 1981 and 1982**

| Years | Actual Membership | Predicted Membership | |
|---|---|---|---|
| | GR-2 | GR-1 | GR-2 |
| 1979 | 18 | 00 | 18 |
| 1980 | 19 | 00 | 19 |
| 1981 | 19 | 00 | 19 |
| 1982 | 10 | 00 | 10 |

TABLE 5-12B

| Year | Type of Error | N | Number Correct | Percent Correct | Percent Error |
|---|---|---|---|---|---|
| 1979 | Type-II | 18 | 18 | 100 | 00 |
| 1980 | Type-II | 19 | 19 | 100 | 00 |
| 1981 | Type-II | 19 | 19 | 100 | 00 |
| 1982 | Type-II | 10 | 10 | 100 | 00 |

*Notes*: (i) Type-II represents type II error( refer Chapter III, p. 63).
(ii) N=Total number of observations in the sample.
(iii) GR-1=Failed Group
GR-2=Non-failed Group

classification of these companies since these are the bo: der line cases, though having discriminant scores above cut off point, of which one is not as confident in their group classification as in other cases in the same year in the sample. Another important observation is that most of the companies in the sample are having low discriminant value in the year 1982 compared to the years 1979, 1980 and 1981. The factors responsible for the low discriminant scores of most of the firms in the sample in the year 1982 are that the jute industry as a whole was affected by the acute recession in the jute market and to some extent the operations of few firms were also affected by workers' strike, lock out, go slow tactics of workers, low demand of jute carpets abroad, frequent heavy load sheddings.

### 5.2.4 *Additional Sample of Non-failed/Non-sick Paper Companies*

30 non-failed paper companies (Appendix M-5) were selected at random irrespective of size and age from the list of paper companies appearing in the Bombay Stock Exchange Directory in the year 1982. The required financial variables of three years (i.e. 1980, 1981 and 1982) of each firm in the sample were collected. The Y-score values of each company for three years are computed by using the discriminant function i.e. $Y = 19.8927V_9 + .0047_{25} + .7141V_{31} + .4860V_{35}$ (refer Chapter IV, pp. 88-89) and presented below in Table 5-13.

TABLE 5-13. **Y-Score Values of Non-Sick Paper Companies for the years 1980, 1981 and 1982**

| Co. Code No. | Years | | |
|---|---|---|---|
| | 1980 | 1981 | 1982 |
| NFP-01 | 2.6953 | 3.6551 | 4.1038 |
| NFP-02 | 5.0833 | 4.7294 | 3.9240 |
| NFP-03 | 4.5849 | 4.1920 | 4.0586 |
| NFP-04 | 3.5289 | 3.2009 | NA |
| NFP-05 | 3.1040 | 2.3820 | 2.4607 |
| NFP-06 | 1.8470 | 2.9269 | 2.8350 |
| NFP-07 | 2.9091 | 1.7755 | —0.2433*S |
| NFP-08 | NA | 2.0629 | 1.9796 |
| NFP-09 | 2.5937 | 2.1944 | 0.0654*S |
| NFP-10 | 3.5669 | 3.2181 | 1.9647 |
| NFP-11 | 2.5248 | 2.8494 | 3.2126 |
| NFP-12 | 2.7411 | 1.9565 | 2.5873 |
| NFP-13 | 6.6787 | 5.8122 | 4.6407 |

TABLE 5-13 (*Contd.*)

| Co. Code No. | Years | | |
|---|---|---|---|
| | 1980 | 1981 | 1982 |
| NFP-14 | NA | 1.4844 | 1.8185 |
| NFP-15 | 4.5036 | 4.0482 | 2.4820 |
| NFP-16 | 4.2824 | 3.5086 | 3.1571 |
| NFP-17 | 1.7512 | 2.7708 | 1.4498 |
| NFP-18 | 2.8998 | 2.3717 | 2.5906 |
| NFP-19 | 5.1235 | 2.5522 | 1.8924 |
| NFP-20 | 4.4142 | 3.5328 | 1.5196 |
| NFP-21 | 4.1046 | 3.2519 | 3.0518 |
| NFP-22 | 6.3166 | 2.7375 | 2.8087 |
| NFP-23 | 1.7166 | 6.2140 | 1.7046 |
| NFP-24 | 5.8418 | 4.6001 | 3.9342 |
| NFP-25 | 2.1652 | 1.4839 | 0.6564*S |
| NFP-26 | 2.3001 | 1.7413 | 1.7841 |
| NFP-27 | 4.2642 | 2.8387 | 2.5237 |
| NFP-28 | 3.6922 | 3.9229 | 1.9986 |
| FFP-29 | 2.7091 | 3.6422 | 4.1264 |
| NFP-30 | 4.0273 | 4.0014 | 2.6717 |

*Notes*: (i) NFP represents non-failed paper company and the digits 1-19 denote the serial number of units in the sample.
(ii) The misclassified companies are marked with*
(iii) The workers' strike is denoted by S.
(iv) The strike year is considered an abnormal year and thus, not included in the accuracy matrix for calculating the predictive accuracy of the model.
(v) Non-availability of data of a firm is denoted by (N.A.).

The accuracy matrix is prepared by using the cut off point (i.e. $Y_c = 1.425$) and shown in Table 5-14.

TABLE 5-14A **Accuracy Matrix of Non-Sick Paper Companies for the years 1980, 1981 and 1982**

| Years | Actual Membership | Predicted Membership | |
|---|---|---|---|
| | GR-2 | GR-1 | GR-2 |
| 1980 | 28 | 00 | 28 |
| 1981 | 30 | 00 | 30 |
| 1982 | 26 | 00 | 26 |

TABLE 5-14B.

| Years | Type of Error | N | Number Correct | Percent Correct | Percent Error |
|---|---|---|---|---|---|
| 1980 | Type-II | 28 | 28 | 100 | 00 |
| 1981 | Type-II | 30 | 30 | 100 | 00 |
| 1982 | Type-II | 26 | 26 | 100 | 00 |

*Notes*: (i) Type-II represents type-II error (refer Chapter III, p. 63)
(ii) N=Total number of observations in the sample
(iii) GR-1=Sick Group
GR-2=Non-Sick Group.

The analysis of the results presented in the accuracy matrix indicates that the discriminant model is very accurate in predicting the chances of survival or failure i.e. financial status of paper companies in the sample. The group classification decision in the case of firms' number NFP-17 and NFP-20 in the year 1982; NFP-14 and NFP-25 in the year 1981 is not as definite as in the case of other firms in the sample, because the Y-score values of these firms fall in the area of 'Zone of Ignorance'. Thus, the probability of belonging of these firms to each of the two groups is to be calculated and further examination is to be made before taking any decision regarding the financial status of these firms.

### 5.2.5 *Additional Sample of Non-Failed/Non-Sick Chemical and Pharmaceutical Companies*

This sample consists of 21 successfully running chemical and pharmaceutical companies (Appendix M-6) selected at random from the list of chemical companies appearing in the Bombay Stock Exchange Directory in the year 1982. The required financial data of three years (i.e. 1980, 1981 and 1982) were collected from the annual reports of these companies. By using the parameters of the model, the Y-score values of each firm for each year are computed and presented below in Table 5-15:

TABLE 5.15 **Y-Score Values of Non-Sick Chemical and Pharmaceutical Companies for the years 1980, 1981 and 1982**

| Co. Code No. | Years | | |
|---|---|---|---|
| | 1980 | 1981 | 1982 |
| NFCP-01 | 3.9602 | 2.4204 | 3.4622 |
| NFCP-02 | 5.3282 | 3.9272 | 2.9471 |
| NFCP-03 | 3.5396 | 2.8967 | 2.4276 |
| NFCP-04 | 5.3632 | 4.6011 | 4.4755 |
| NFCP-05 | 7.3052 | 4.3061 | 2.4363 |
| NFCP-06 | 4.2247 | 4.3282 | 4.1336 |
| NFCP-07 | 3.6905 | 5.1698 | 6.1003 |
| NFCP-08 | 5.3493 | 4.0043 | 2.3701 |
| NFCP-09 | 6.9955 | 6.4468 | 6.6719 |
| NFCP-10 | 3.1772 | 2.8627 | 0.8371*S |
| NFCP-11 | 3.1192 | 3.0494 | 2.8169 |
| NGCP-12 | 3.3558 | 3.2475 | 3.2824 |
| NFCP-13 | 2.7362 | 5.9622 | 4.5160 |
| NFCP-14 | 2.9194 | 3.3013 | 3.7002 |
| NFCP-15 | 4.8497 | 3.7323 | 3.4072 |
| NFCP-16 | 6.6976 | 6.3729 | 4.2226 |

| Co. Code No. | Years | | |
|---|---|---|---|
| | 1910 | 1981 | 1982 |
| NFCP-17 | 3.7191 | 2.5622 | 1.6026 |
| NFCP-18 | 2.2200 | 2.1304 | 4.6950 |
| NFCP-19 | 2.5935 | 2.7925 | 3.5099 |
| NFCP-20 | 4.4133 | 3.0365 | 2.7506 |
| NFCP-21 | 4.6056 | 4.4931 | 3.2253 |

*Notes* : (i) The misclassified firms are marked with*.
(ii) S represents the workers' strike or lock out in the factory.
(iii) Strike year scores are not included in the accuracy matrix being abnormal year.
(iv) NFCP represents the non-failed chemical and Pharmaceutical Company and 1-21 denotes the serial number of companies in the sample.

By using the cut off point ($Y_c = 1.425$), the companies in the sample are classified to one of the groups and presented below in the form of a accuracy matrix in Table 5-16.

The analysis of results in Table 5-16 clearly brings out that all the units in the sample are correctly classified in all the years which indicates a very high degree of accuracy of the model in predicting the financial status of chemical companies

TABLE 5-16A. **Accuracy Matrix of Non-Sick Chemical and Pharmaceutical Companies for the years 1980, 1981 and 1982**

| Years | Actual Membership | Predicted Membership | |
|---|---|---|---|
| | GR-2 | GR-1 | GR-2 |
| 1980 | 21 | 00 | 21 |
| 1981 | 21 | 00 | 21 |
| 1982 | 20 | 00 | 20 |

TABLE 5-16B.

| Years | Type of Error | N | Number Correct | Percent Correct | Percent Error |
|---|---|---|---|---|---|
| 1980 | Type-II | 21 | 21 | 100 | 00 |
| 1981 | Tyep-II | 21 | 21 | 100 | 00 |
| 1982 | Type-II | 20 | 20 | 100 | 00 |

*Notes*: (i) Type-II represents type-II error (refer Chapter III, p. 63).
(ii) N=Total number of observations.
(iii) GR-1=Sick Group
GR-2=Non-Sick Group.

in the sample. Another important observation is that the Y-scores of most of the units in the sample are consistent over a period of three years. It shows that the model is very effective in predicting the financial health of firms in chemical and pharmaceutical industry.

### 5.2.6 *Additional Sample of Non-Sick/Non-Failed Iron and Steel Companies*

20 non-failed/non-sick iron and steel units (Appendix M-7) were taken at random from the Bombay Stock Exchange Directory and the relevant financial data for a period of three years (i.e. 1980, 1981 and 1982) were collected from the annual reports of these companies By usin the discriminant function i e. $Y=19.8927V_9+0.0047V_{25}+0.7141V_{31}+0.4860V_{35}$ (refer Chapter IV, pp. 88-89) the discriminant scores of each firm for each year are computed and shown in Table 5-17:

From the Table 5-17, the accuracy matrix is prepared by taking cut off point (i.e $Y_c=1.425$) as membership classification criteria and presented in the form of a accuracy matrix in Table 5-18:

The analysis of the results indicates that the model is very accurate in all the three years in predicting the financial health of iron and steel units in the sample. Though all the units in

TABLE 5-17. **Y-Score Values of Non-Sick Iron and Steel Companies for the years 1980, 1981 and 1982**

| Co. Code No. | Years | | |
|---|---|---|---|
| | 1980 | 1981 | 1982 |
| NFIS-01 | 3.7158 | 3.8560 | 3.5552 |
| NFIS-02 | 5.5904 | 3.0556 | 3.5939 |
| NFIS-03 | 4.7928 | 4.2674 | 5.7497 |
| NFIS-04 | 2.9493 | 3.4367 | 2.7892 |
| NFIS-05 | 4.1488 | 4.9412 | 4.8320 |
| NFIS-06 | 4.4294 | 2.2074 | 1.4442 |
| NFIS-07 | 3,6871 | 3.4846 | 2.3071 |
| NFIS-08 | 5.9385 | 4.3319 | 3.2854 |
| NFIS-09 | 1.4270 | 2.1218 | 2.7811 |
| NFIS-10 | 3.2345 | 3.9247 | 3.7748 |
| NFIS-11 | 8.7574 | 12.9496 | NA |
| NFIS-12 | 4.5318 | 4.9271 | —1.4256*S |
| NFIS-13 | 10.0819 | 6.2546 | 2.4262 |
| NFIS-14 | 6.9120 | 5.4309 | 3.0478 |
| NFIS-15 | 8.8698 | 2.6795 | 0.1850** |
| NFIS-16 | 2.6292 | 2.9399 | 3.9896 |
| NFIS-17 | 4.0621 | 4.0733 | 3.2854 |
| NFIS-18 | 0.7029*S | 2.6804 | 2.8851 |
| NFIS-19 | 4.8465 | 2.9572 | 1.8943 |
| NFIS-20 | 4.9967 | 3.2491 | 3.8684 |

*Notes*: (i) NFIS represents non-failed iron and steel company and 1-20 denotes the serial number of companies in the sample.

(ii) The misclassified firms are marked with*.

(iii) The strike in the company is denoted by S.

(iv) **=Factory remained closed for 5½ months on account of fire accident.

(v) The firms marked with S and ** are not included in the accuracy matrix.

(vi) Non-availability of data is denoted by (N.A.).

TABLE 5-18A. **Accuracy Matrix of Non-Sick Iron and Steel Companies for the years 1980, 1981 and 1982**

| Years | Actual Membership | Predicted Membership | |
|---|---|---|---|
| | GR-2 | GR-1 | GR-2 |
| 1980 | 19 | 00 | 19 |
| 1981 | 20 | 00 | 20 |
| 1982 | 17 | 00 | 17 |

TABLE 5.18 B

| Years | Type of Error | N | Number Correct | Percent Correct | Percent Error |
|---|---|---|---|---|---|
| 1980 | Type-II | 19 | 19 | 100 | 00 |
| 1981 | Type-II | 20 | 20 | 100 | 00 |
| 1982 | Type-II | 17 | 17 | 100 | 00 |

*Notes*: (i) Type-II mean type II error (refer Chapter III, p. 63).
(ii) N=Total number of observations.
(iii) GR-1=Sick Group
GR-2=Non-Sick Group.

the sample in all the years are getting Y-scores above the cut off point (i.e. $Y_c=1.425$), however, the probability of belonging of firms' number NFIS-9 in 1980 and NFIS-6 in 1982 to each of the group is to be computed and further examination is to be made in order to determine the financial status of these firms with more confidence, since the Y-score of these firms fall in the 'Zone of Ignorance' of which the classification is not as definite as in other cases getting Y-score beyond the 'Zone of Ignorance'.

### 5.2.7 *Additional Sample of Non-Failed/Non-Sick General Engineering Companies*

This sample consists of 21 non-sick/non-failed general

engineering units (Appendix M-8) taken at random from the list of companies appearing in the Bombay Stock Exchange Directory. Three years (i.e. 1980, 1981 and 1982) financial data were collected from the annual reports of these companies. The Y-score values of each company for each year are computed by using the discriminant function i.e. $Y=19.8927V_9 +0.0047V_{25}+0.714LV_{31}+0.4860V_{35}$ (refer Chapter IV, pp. 88-89) presented in Table 5-19:

Using the cut off point (i.e. $Y_c=1.425$), the units are classified into one of the groups and presented in Table 5-20.

The Table 5-20 clearly indicates that the model is very accurate in all the three years in predicting the financial health of general engineering units in the sample. Further analysis reveals that the discriminant scores of company number NFGE-20 in 1980 and NFGE-04 in 1982 falls in the 'Zone of Ignorance' (1.33—1.52) of which no definite membership classification decision can be taken. Thus, the probability of belonging of company number NFGE-20 and NFGE-4 to each of the two groups is to be calculated before making any definite group classification decision of these firms.

### 5.2.8 *Additional Sample of Non-Sick/Non-Failed Sugar Companies*

A sample of 21 successfully running sugar units (Appendix M-9) was taken at random from the Bombay Stock Exchange Directory and financial data of three years (i.e 1980, 1981 and 1982) were collected. Using the parameters established in discriminant model i e. $Y=19.8927V_9+0.0047V_{25}+0.7141V_{31}+ 0.4860V_{35}$ (refer Chapter IV, pp. 88-89), the discriminant scores of each company for each year are worked out and presented in Table 5-21.

On the basis of the cut off point (i.e. $Y_e=1.425$) as determined in the initial sample, the predictive accuracy of the model is ascertained and shown in Table 5-22.

The analysis of results in Table 5-22 clearly points out that all the units are correctly classified in all the years which amount to a very high degree of accuracy in predicting the financial health of firms in sugar industry. However, the

TABLE 5-19. **Y-Score Values of Non-Sick General Engineering Companies for the years 1980, 1981 and 1982**

| Co. Code No. | Years | | |
|---|---|---|---|
| | 1980 | 1981 | 1982 |
| NFGE-01 | 1.9700 | 2.1906 | 2.7807 |
| NFGE-02 | 5.6675 | 5.6821 | 5.3202 |
| NFGE-03 | 5.2958 | 8.5894 | 4.4254 |
| NFGE-04 | 2.8716 | 3.4442 | 1.4961 |
| NFGE-05 | 4.4943 | 4.0478 | 3.6768 |
| NFGE-06 | 7.3724 | 3.9823 | 3.1447 |
| NFGE-07 | 3.7418 | 2.8111 | 3.6429 |
| NFGE-08 | 2.7972 | 2.7429 | 2.8475 |
| NFGE-09 | 2.5482 | 3.8797 | 3.4904 |
| NFGE-10 | 5.4482 | 4.7071 | 3.0913 |
| NFGE-11 | 3.0389 | 3.6158 | 2.7321 |
| NFGE-12 | 3.7680 | 2.1921 | 3.0510 |
| NFGE-13 | 5.5431 | 5.3787 | 3.5072 |
| NFGE-14 | 2.2430 | 6.1506 | 4.5280 |
| NFGE-15 | 1.5742 | 2.7209 | 5.6895 |
| NFGE-16 | 2.2690 | 3.1664 | 3.3852 |
| NFGE-17 | 3.4210 | 3.0338 | 1.2707*S |
| NFGE-18 | 4.2182 | 4.0872 | 3.3722 |
| NFGE-19 | 3.9863 | 4.2332 | 3.4776 |
| NFGE-20 | 1.5291 | 2.0105 | 3.9245 |
| NFGE-21 | 3.9469 | 4.7563 | 4.1075 |

*Notes:* (i) NFGE represents the non-failed general engineering company and 1-21 denotes the serial number of companies in the sample.

(ii) The misclassified units are marked with*.

(iii) S denotes the strike in the company.

(iv) The firm score marked with S is not included in the accuracy matrix.

TABLE 5-20A. **Accuracy Matrix of Non-Sick General Engineering Companies for the years 1980, 1981 and 1982**

| Years | Actual Membership | Predicted Membership | |
|---|---|---|---|
| | GR-2 | GR-1 | GR-2 |
| 1980 | 21 | 00 | 100 |
| 1981 | 21 | 00 | 100 |
| 1982 | 20 | 00 | 100 |

TABLE 5-20B

| Years | Type of Error | N | Number Correct | Percent Correct | Percent Error |
|---|---|---|---|---|---|
| 1980 | Type-II | 21 | 21 | 100 | 00 |
| 1981 | Type-II | 21 | 21 | 100 | 00 |
| 1982 | Type-II | 20 | 20 | 100 | 00 |

*Notes*: (i) Type-II represents type-II error (refer Chapter III, p. 63).
(ii) N=Total number of units in the sample.
(iii) GR-1=Sick Group
GR-2=Non-Sick Group

probability of belonging of firm number NFS-8 is to be worked out before classifying the firm to one of the group on the basis of Y-score which falls in the area of 'Zone of Ignorance' (1.33—1.52).

### 5.2.9 *Additional Sample of Non-Failed/Non-Sick Electrical Companies*

This sample contains 20 non-failed electrical units (Appendix M-10) taken at random from the list of electrical companies in Bombay Stock Exchange Directory and three years (i.e. 1980,

TABLE 5-21. **Y-Score Values of Non-Sick Sugar Companies for the years 1980, 1981 and 1982**

| Co. Code No. | Years 1980 | 1981 | 1982 |
|---|---|---|---|
| NFS-01 | 4.2286 | 3.1251 | 2.5476 |
| NFS-02 | 6.3038 | 1.8389 | 1.7829 |
| NFS-03 | 3.5764 | 3.9818 | 3.4422 |
| NFS-04 | 5.2003 | 1.8226 | 1.6232 |
| NFS-05 | 5.3247 | 3.3274 | —3.6152*S |
| NFS-06 | 4.0706 | 2.3858 | 2.2273 |
| NFS-07 | 3.3204 | 2.9164 | 2.7935 |
| NFS-08 | 2.5686 | 2.3839 | 1.5409 |
| NFS-09 | 3.3468 | 4.0712 | 3.3783 |
| NFS-10 | 1.9143 | 2.8665 | 1.6372 |
| NFS-11 | 4.5472 | 4.8158 | 4.0164 |
| NFS-12 | 6.0395 | 2.6931 | 3.8082 |
| NFS-13 | 4.6647 | 3.5147 | 2.0198 |
| NFS-14 | 5.5753 | 2.1913 | 2.4171 |
| NFS-15 | 3.0962 | 3.3101 | 2.3358 |
| NFS-16 | 4.7162 | 4.1026 | 3.0800 |
| NFS-17 | 7.2191 | 3.8900 | 3.6020 |
| NFS-18 | 3.0255 | 2.9348 | 4.0328 |
| NFS-19 | 4.5531 | 7.5806 | 3.8613 |
| NFS-20 | 7.7009 | 5.7722 | 2.8511 |
| NFS-21 | 3.2812 | 2.3487 | 2.4986 |

*Notes*: (i) The misclassified firm is marked with*.
(ii) The strike year in the factory is denoted by S.
(iii) The strike year is not included in the accuracy matrix.
(iv) NFS 1-20 represents the non-failed sugar companies and their serial number in the sample.

TABLE 5-22A. **Accuracy Matrix of Non-Sick Sugar Companies for the years 1980, 1981 and 1982**

| Years | Actual Membership | Predicted Membership | |
|---|---|---|---|
| | GR-2 | GR-1 | GR-2 |
| 1980 | 21 | 00 | 21 |
| 1981 | 21 | 00 | 21 |
| 1982 | 20 | 00 | 20 |

TABLE 5-22B

| Years | Type of Error | N | Number Correct | Percent Correct | Percent Error |
|---|---|---|---|---|---|
| 1980 | Type-II | 21 | 21 | 100 | 00 |
| 1981 | Type-II | 21 | 21 | 100 | 00 |
| 1982 | Type-II | 20 | 20 | 100 | 00 |

*Notes*: (i) Type-II represent type-II error (refer Chapter III, p. 63),
(ii) N=Total number of units in the sample.
(iii) GR-1=Sick Group
GR-2=Non-Sick Group.

1981, 1982) financial data were collected from the annual reports of these companies. The discriminant scores are worked out by using the parameters of discriminant function i.e. $Y=19.8927V_9+0.0047V_{25}+0.7141V_{31}+0.4860V_{35}$ (refer Chapter IV, pp. 88-89) and shown in Table 5-23.

Using the cut off point ($Y_c=1.425$), the predictive accuracy of the model is ascertained and shown in the form of a accuracy matrix in Table 5-24.

The results presented in Table 5-24 clearly indicates that all the units are correctly classified in all the three years by the discriminant model. Another important observation is that the Y-scores of all the units are above the limits of 'Zone of

TABLE 5-23. **Y-Score Values of Non-Sick Electrical Companies for the years 1980, 1981 and 1982**

| Co. Code No. | Years | | |
|---|---|---|---|
| | 1980 | 1981 | 1982 |
| NFE-01 | 3.3858 | 4.3919 | 3.9385 |
| NFE-02 | 3.7244 | 4.0108 | 3.4254 |
| NFE-03 | 4.8415 | 6.1412 | 3.4520 |
| NFE-04 | 3.9343 | 4.3602 | 4.3723 |
| NFE-05 | 7.9632 | 5.8526 | —3.5158*S |
| NFE-06 | 2.3348 | 1.5433 | 4.2274 |
| NFE-07 | 5.7200 | 4.3979 | 2.7372 |
| NFE-08 | 2.6289 | 3.9453 | 2.6021 |
| NFE-09 | 1.9406 | 1.9258 | 1.9438 |
| NFE-10 | 4.8660 | 7.3602 | 3.8632 |
| NFE-11 | 3.2288 | 4.1223 | 4.4385 |
| NFE-12 | 3.1099 | 3.7174 | 2.4155 |
| NFE-13 | 3.8296 | 4.0835 | 3.7157 |
| MFE-14 | 5.1050 | 6.1372 | 6.0809 |
| NFE-15 | 7.1334 | 5.9148 | 5.1908 |
| NFE-16 | 4.6521 | 5.5624 | 3.6063 |
| NFE-17 | 17.1686 | 5.5895 | 4.8949 |
| NFE-18 | 3.9355 | 2.6726 | 3.0502 |
| NFE-19 | 3.9049 | 3.8772 | 3.3103 |
| NFE-20 | 3.0527 | 3.5329 | 3.0630 |

*Notes*: (i) The misclassified unit is marked with*.
(ii) The strike in the factory is denoted by S.
(iii) The strike year score is not included in the accuracy matrix.
(iv) NFE 1-20 denotes the non-failed electrical units and their serial number in the sample.

TABLE 5-24A. **Accuracy Matrix of Non-Sick Electrical Companies for the years 1980, 1981 and 1982**

| Years | Actual Membership | Predicted Membership | |
|---|---|---|---|
| | GR-2 | GR-1 | GR-2 |
| 1980 | 20 | 00 | 20 |
| 1981 | 20 | 00 | 20 |
| 1982 | 19 | 00 | 19 |

TABLE 5-24B.

| Years | Type of Error | N | Number Correct | Percent Correct | Percent Error |
|---|---|---|---|---|---|
| 1980 | Type-II | 20 | 20 | 100 | C0 |
| 1981 | Type-II | 20 | 20 | 100 | 00 |
| 1982 | Type-II | 19 | 19 | 100 | 00 |

*Notes*: (i) Type-II represents type-II error (refer Chapter III, p. 63).
(ii) N=Total number of units.
(iii) GR-1=Sick Group
GR-2=Non-Sick Group.

Ignorance' (i.e. 1.33-1.52) which clearly illustrates that the model is very effective in predicting the financial health of electrical units.

5.2.10 *Additional Sample of Non-Failed Rubber Units*

A sample of 10 non-failed rubber units (Appendix M-11) was taken at random from the Bombay Stock Exchange Directory. A small sample of only 10 rubber units was taken on account of non-availability of financial data of more number of companies. Financial data of three years (i.e. 1980, 1981 and 1982) were collected. The discriminant scores are computed by using the discriminant function i.e. $Y = 19.8927V_9 + 0.0047V_{25} + 0.7141V_{31} + 0.4860V_{35}$ (refer Chapter IV, pp. 88-89) and shown below in Table 5-25.

TABLE 5-25. **Y-Score Values of Non-Sick Rubber Companies for the years 1980, 1981 and 1982**

| Co. Code No. | Years | | |
|---|---|---|---|
| | 1980 | 1981 | 1982 |
| NFR-01 | 8.5090 | 5.4859 | 5.9523 |
| NFR-02 | 4.1692 | 5.7936 | 6.0986 |
| NFR-03 | 4.5243 | 3.9440 | 4.4384 |
| NFR-04 | 1.7291 | 2.9053 | 1.7877 |
| NFR-05 | 6.6347 | 7.7705 | 6.8798 |
| NFR-06 | NA | 6.0128 | 4.7802 |
| NFR-07 | 4.5920 | 4.8648 | 4.5169 |
| NFR-08 | 7.5356 | 6.4205 | 5.4627 |
| NFR-09 | 2.9009 | 4.2260 | 4.1391 |
| NFR-10 | 1.4227 | 3.1953 | 2.4906 |

*Notes*: (i) N.A. represents non-availability of data.
(ii) NFR 1-10 represents the non-failed rubber units and their serial number in the sample.

The accuracy of the model is ascertained by classifying the companies into one of the groups on the basis of cut off point ($Y_c = 1.425$) and shown in Table 5-26:

Table 5-26 indicates that all the units in the sample are correctly classified in all the three years which shows a high degree of accuracy of the model in predicting the financial status of the firms in rubber industry. Though firm number NFR-10 Y-score is above the cut off point (i.e. $Y_c = 1.425$), however, the probability of firm's belonging to each of the two groups is to be calculated before classifying the firm to group-2, because the Y-score of this firm falls within the 'Zone of Ignorance' of which one is not as confident as in other cases

TABLE 5-26A. **Accuracy Matrix of Non-Sick Rubber Companies for the years 1980, 1981 and 1982**

| Years | Actual Membership | Predicted Membership | |
|---|---|---|---|
| | GR-2 | GR-1 | GR-2 |
| 1980 | 09 | 00 | 09 |
| 1981 | 10 | 00 | 10 |
| 1982 | 10 | 00 | 10 |

TABLE 5-26B

| Years | Type of Error | N | Number Correct | Percent Correct | Percent Error |
|---|---|---|---|---|---|
| 1980 | Type-II | 09 | 09 | 100 | 00 |
| 1981 | Type-II | 10 | 10 | 100 | 00 |
| 1982 | Type-II | 10 | 10 | 100 | 00 |

*Notes*: (i) Type-II represents type-II error (refer Chapter III, p. 63).
(ii) N=Number of units in the sample.
(iii) GR-1=Sick Group.
GR-2=Non-Sick Group.

whose discriminant scores fall beyond the 'Zone of Ignorance' in making group classification decision.

CHAPTER VI

# Summary, Conclusions and Directions for Further Research

Despite the voluminous literature built up on financial ratios, the principles of such analysis have lacked scientific approach. Different authors have used different models to emphasize the role of these ratios in identifying the sickness in companies. The present study seeks:

(a) to assess the quality of financial ratios as an analytical technique to evaluate the performance of business enterprises; and
(b) to verify the widely held beliefs in accounting literature regarding the comparative utility of various financial ratios.

An attempt has also been made to systematically analyse the role of financial ratios and to develop a multi-ratio model performing the best overall job in the prediction of corporate failure/sickness.

The major conclusions of the study are summarised below:

Most of the studies dealing with corporate failure/sickness have explored the number of financial ratios as predictors of corporate failure and incorporated a large number of ratios in their predictive models. Their conclusions, however, differ regarding the question of which ratio or set of ratios perform well as indicators of corporate failure/sickness and thus, each model requires further verification under different business environments.

Thirty six financial ratios have been empirically tested in this case univariately as well multivariately on a sample of 78 companies (39 failed companies and 39 non-failed companies). The empirical results on the basis of a univariate technique known as 'Dichotomous classification test' have shown that financial ratios taken individually can predict the corporate failure/sickness. But not all ratios predict equally well. There is relative difference in the predictive power of financial ratios. The cash-flow to total tangible assets ratio has been found possessing the highest predictive power followed by the earning before interest and taxes to total tangible assets ratio. Among the solvency and liquidity ratios, solvency ratios are found to be more reliable predictors of corporate health than the liquidity ratios. The empirical results indicate that companies with heavy debt and inadequate equity base are more prone to failure/sickness. All liquidity ratios proved to be very poor in predicting corporate health. The current ratio ($V_{25}$) and quick ratio ($V_{24}$) have resulted in almost three and a half times more classification error (refer Table 4-2, pp. 118-20) than the best profitability ratio. It contradicts the considerable importance traditionally attached to liquidity ratios in appraising corporate health. The net cash flow from operations to the reservoir has been found the most crucial factor, while the size of the reservoir is the least important factor in detecting the potential corporate failure/sickness.

A multi-ratio discriminant model has been developed containing four independent ratios serving as the best predictive variables by using various statistical techniques known as t-test, factor analysis and the discriminant analysis. The best discriminant function investigated is as under:

$$Y = 19.8927V_9 + 0.0047V_{25} + 0.7141V_{31} + 0.4860V_{35}$$

where

$Y$ = Overall discriminant score

$V_9$ = Earning before Interest and Taxes/Total Tangible Assets

$V_{25}$ = Current Assets/Current Liabilities

$V_{31}$ = Net Sales/Total Tangible Assets

$V_{35}$ = Defensive Assets/Total Operating Expenditures. This ratio is known as 'Defensive Interval Ratio'.

The discriminant model so developed is not always optimal since the process is iterative, it, however, does the best job among the alternatives which involves numerous computer runs and analysis of various ratio-profiles. The set of variables in the above discriminant function are independent and least correlated with each other in both the groups, namely, failed group and non-failed group (refer Table 4-8, p. 89) and thus each variable provides additional information about the financial health of a company. The contribution of each variable is additional towards the predictive power of the discriminant model.

The discriminant score $Y_c = 1.425$ has been determined as the optimum value (i.e. the best cut off point) to classify the firms either into potentially failed/sick or non-failed/non-sick group of companies. If the individual discriminant score of any company is below $Y_c = 1.425$, it is to be classified as a potentially failed/sick company and vice-versa. The accuracy of the model amounts to 95 per cent, 86 per cent, 82 per cent 79 per cent and 78 per cent in predicting corporate failure in the initial sample one to six years respectively prior to failure. It shows that the model is very accurate in predicting the corporate failure, though with decreasing probability.

The probability of misclassification of the model is also ascertained in order to judge the reliability of accuracy of the model more rigorously. The probability of misclassification of the model is $P_{g1} = 0.1131$ and $P_{g2} = 0.1292$ for failed companies and non-failed companies respectively where $P_{g1}$ represents the probability of misclassification for companies in Group-1 and $P_{g2}$ represents the probability of misclassification for companies in Group-2. The term misclassification in this context means that assignment of companies to failed or non-failed group on the basis of the model is expected to disagree with the actual or a *priori* classification in 11.31 per cent and 12.92 per cent cases in Group-1 and Group-2 respectively. It means that further examination may be required only in 11.31 per cent firms in Group-1 and 12.92 per cent firms in Group-2 in order to classify them correctly.

The area falling between 1.33 to 1.52 discriminant scores is defined as the 'Zone of Ignorance' or area of uncertainty' because of susceptibility to misclassification. Since errors are observed in this range of values, there will be uncertainty about a new firm whose Y-score value falls within the 'Zone of Uncertainty'. Hence, the probability of misclassification of each company falling within the 'Zone of Uncertainty', should be ascertained (refer Chapter IV, pp. 105-106) and used as an additional aid alongwith the discriminant scores in predicting their chances of survival or failure.

For prediction purposes, the model has been applied to additional samples taken from both homogeneous and non-homogeneous group of industries. To verify the reliability and effectiveness of the model, a series of additional samples of failed and non-failed companies have been introduced and the classification error rates ascertained by using the parameters of the model established in the initial sample. The model proved to be very accurate in classifying the firms contained in additional samples. The Table 6-1 given below shows the overall performance of the model in predicting corporate failure/sickness.

TABLE 6-1. **Overall Predictive Accuracy of the Model**

| Year Prior to Failure | In Initial Sample | In Additional Samples | |
|---|---|---|---|
| | Non-Homogeneous Firms % | Non-Homogeneous Firms % | Homogeneous Firms % |
| 1 | 95.00 | 95.83 | 99.00 |
| 2 | 87.00 | 95.83 | 97.22 |
| 3 | 86.00 | 90.48 | 97.14 |
| 4 | 82.00 | 93.75 | 93.94 |
| 5 | 79.00 | 86.67 | 90.91 |
| 6 | 78.00 | 86.67 | 87.09 |

Table 6-1 indicates that the model is very accurate in predicting the corporate failure in both homogeneous and non-homogeneous group of industries, though with decreasing probability. The fall in the accuracy of the model is logically understandable taking into account the long period that has elapsed, because the indicators (ratios) of failure become less and less clear as the lead time from the date of event (failure) increases. Secondly, the model has been found more effective in case of homogeneous group of industries compared with non-homogeneous companies which may, in some measure, be due to the homogeneity of the industry group to which it has been applied.

It is seen from Table 6-2 that the model seems to be reliable and comprehensive in predicting corporate failure/sickness in comparison with the most widely discussed studies—Altman, Beaver, Deakin, Marc Blum—in this area. The year to year figures of precentage error show remarkable consistency, unlike Altman's and others' model. The percentage classification error in predicting corporate failure/sickness of the above studies along with the predicted results of this model are summarised in Table 6-2:

## Applications of the Model

It is evident that the model predicts corporate failure/sickness several years in advance, though with decreasing probability. Such a warning system obviously has important uses for the management, lenders and investors:

First, the model, if used periodically to assess the firm's position, has the ability to predict corporate problems early enough so as to enable management to realize the gravity of situation in time and take timely action to stem further sickness.

Second, the lenders—commercial banks and other lending institutions—may use the failure prediction model in the process of credit evaluation. The model will assist the lenders to classify the borrowing units into a potentially sick or sound category. However, it should not be used as the only means of credit evaluation. The other important non-accounting variables such as the purpose of the loan, its maturity, the security involved and the deposit status of the applicant should be considered alongwith the Y-score (i.e. discriminant score) of the borrowing unit. It should be used as a guide in efforts to

TABLE 6-2. **Classification Error Rates for Predicting Failure/Bankruptcy**

*(Percentage Error)*

| Year Before Failure/ Bankruptcy | Beaver's best ratio (cashflow/ Total debt) | Altman's Discriminant Function | Edward Deakin's Model | Marc P. Blum's FCM | Our Model | | |
|---|---|---|---|---|---|---|---|
| | | | | | In Initial Sample | In Additional Samples | |
| | | | | | Non-Homogeneous Group | Non-Homogeneous Group | Homogeneous Group |
| 1 | 13.00 | 05.00 | 03.00 | 07.00 | 05.00 | 04.17 | 00.01 |
| 2 | 21.00 | 28.00 | 04.50 | 20.00 | 13.00 | 04.17 | 02.78 |
| 3 | 23.00 | 52.00 | 04.50 | 30.00 | 14.00 | 09.52 | 02.86 |
| 4 | 24.00 | 71.00 | 21.00 | N.A. | 18.00 | 06.25 | 06.06 |
| 5 | 22.00 | 64.00 | 17.00 | N.A. | 21.00 | 13.33 | 09.09 |
| 6 | N.A. | N.A. | N.A. | N.A. | 22.00 | 13.33 | 12.91 |

lower the cost of investigation of loan applicants. It may also be used for evaluating the repayment behaviour of a borrower. It will assist the lending institutions in monitoring the concerns which have already been granted loans by taking timely actions. The early stages of sickness, if detected, will enable the lending institutions to tighten their grip of inspections to force the units to improve their performance.

Third, the model may be used by potential investors for screening out undesirable investments. Since the model is basically predictive, the investors may use it for portfolio selection.

## Directions for Further Research

Although financial ratio analysis in the model developed shows a high degree of accuracy, it is, therefore, necessary to emphasize that continuing research is also needed in this area to achieve greater refinement. At this point, there appears to be scope for further research in the following areas:

(a) Perhaps the most important area for further research is to extend the model to public sector units, private limited companies and unincorporated entities. An attempt can also be made to extend the analysis to relatively smaller firms, where the incidence of failure is greater than big corporations.

(b) The inclusion of non financial measures like operational and technical parameters might improve the results of the present study. A combination of operational, technical and financial parameters may prove better indicator between the sick and healthy units for early detection of sickness. Thus, further research incorporating the impact of these factors may be conducted.

(c) A study incorporating the market rate of return (dividend plus price changes) and the variability in financial ratios over time as predictors of failure may improve the results of the present study.

(d) The research in the direction of analysing the impact of price level adjustments on predictive ability of financial ratios is also called for.

# Appendices

## *APPENDIX A*

### Beaver's List of Financial Ratios

**Group I (Cash Flow Ratios)**

1. Cash Flow to Sales
2. Cash Flow to Total Assets
3. Cash Flow to Net Worth
4. Cash Flow to Total Debt

**Group II (Net Income Ratios)**

1. Net Income to Sales
2. Net Income to Total Assets
3. Net Income to Net Worth
4. Net Income to Total Debt

**Group III (Debt to Total Asset Ratios)**

1. Current Liabilities to Total Assets
2. Long Term Liabilities to Total Assets
3. Current plus Long Term Liabilities to Total Assets
4. Current plus Long Term plus Preferred Stock to Total Assets

**Group IV (Liquid Asset to Total Asset Ratios)**

1. Cash to Total Assets
2. Quick Assets to Total Assets
3. Current Assets to Total Assets
4. Working Capital to Total Assets

**Group V (Liquid-Asset to Current Debt Ratios)**

1. Cash to Current Liabilities
2. Quick Assets to Current Liabilities
3. Current Assets to Current Liabilities

**Group VI (Turnover Ratios)**

1. Cash to Sales
2. Accounts Receivables to Sales
3. Inventory to Sales
4. Quick Assets to Sales
5. Current Assets to Sales
6. Working Capital to Sales
7. Net Worth to Sales
8. Total Assets to Sales
9. Cash Interval (Cash to Fund Expenditures for Operations)
10. Defensive Interval (Defensive Assets to Fund Expenditures for Operations)
11. No Credit Interval (Defensive Assets Minus Current Liabilities to Fund Expenditures for Operations)

---

*Source*: William, H. Beaver, 'Financial Ratios As Predictors of Failure', Empirical Research in Accounting: Selected Studies 1966, Supplement to Vol. 4, *Journal of Accounting Research*, p. 78.

*APPENDIX B*

## Altman's List of Variables Explaining Corporate Failure

1. $X_1$=Return on Assets (Earning before Interest and Taxes to Total Assets)
2. $X_2$=Stability of Earnings (Measured by the normalized measure of standard error of estimate around a ten year trend in $X_1$)
3. $X_3$=Debt Service (Earning before Interest and Taxes to Total Interest Payment)
4. $X_4$=Cummulative Profitability (Retained earnings to Total Assets)
5. $X_5$=Liquidity (Current Assets to Current Liabilities)
6. $X_6$=Capitalization (Equity to Total Capital)
7. $X_7$=Size (Measured by Total Assets)

---

*Source*: Altman, Haldman and Narayanan, *Journal of Banking and Finance*, June 1977.

## *APPENDIX C*

### Deakin's Percentage Error for 14 Ratios on Dichotomous Classification Test

| Ratio | Year Before Failure | | |
|---|---|---|---|
| | 1st Year | 3rd Year | 5th Year |
| 1. CF/TD | 20 | 28 | 27 |
| 2. NI/TA | 27 | 30 | 38 |
| 3. TD/TA | 20 | 22 | 33 |
| 4. CA/TA | 36 | 41 | 47 |
| 5. QA/TA | 34 | 47 | 52 |
| 6. WC/TA | 30 | 34 | 34 |
| 7. Cash/TA | 33 | 47 | 47 |
| 8. CA/CL | 28 | 25 | 41 |
| 9. QA/CL | 30 | 41 | 44 |
| 10. Cash/CL | 36 | 36 | 41 |
| 11. CA/Sales | 48 | 52 | 50 |
| 12. QA/Sales | 52 | 55 | 53 |
| 13. WC/Sales | 28 | 45 | 47 |
| 14. Cash/Sales | 47 | 52 | 48 |

*Source:* Deakin, *Journal of Accounting Research*, Vol. I, No. 10, Spring, 1972, p. 169.

## *APPENDIX D*

### **Deakin's Percentage Error Rates on Discriminant Analysis Test**

| Year Before Failure | Initial Sample | Hold Out Sample |
|---|---|---|
| | Percentage Error Rates | Percentage Error Rates |
| 1. | 03.0 | 22.0 |
| 2. | 04.5 | 06.0 |
| 3. | 04.5 | 12.0 |
| 4. | 21.0 | 23.0 |
| 5. | 17.0 | 15.0 |

*Source*: Deakin, *Jonrnal of Accounting Research*, Spring, 1972.

*APPENDIX E*

## Blum's Failing Company Model

I. *Liquidity*

A. Short-Run Liquidity
Flow: 1. The Quick Flow Ratio
Position: 2. Net Quick Assets/Inventory

B. Long-Run Liquidity
Flow: 3. Cash Flow/Total Liabilities
Position: 4. Net Worth at their Market Value/Total Liabilities
5. Net Worth at Book Value/Total Liabilities

II. *Profitability*

6. Rate of Return to Common Stock Holders who Invest for a minimum of three years

III. *Variability*

7. Standard Deviation of Net Income over a period.
8. Trend Breaks for Net Income
9. Slope for Net Income
10-12. Standard Deviation, Trend Breaks, and Slope of the Ratio, Net Quick Assets to Inventory; Variables 10, 11 and 12 are only used at the first and second year before failure.

*Source*: Blum, M., *Journal of Accounting Research*, Spring, 1974, p. 16.

## *APPENDIX F*

### Ohlson's List of Financial Ratios

| | | |
|---|---|---|
| 1. SIZE | = | Log (Total Assets/GNP Price Level Index) |
| 2. TLTA | = | Total Liabilities Divided by Total Assets |
| 3. WCTA | = | Working Capital Divided by Total Assets |
| 4. CLCA | = | Current Liabilities Divided by Total Assets |
| 5. OENEG | = | One if Total Liabilities Exceed Total Assets, Zero Otherwise |
| 6. NITA | = | Net Income Divided by Total Assets |
| 7. FUTL | = | Funds Provided by Operations Divided by Total Liabilities |
| 8. INTWO | = | One if Net Income was Negative for the two years, Zero otherwise. |
| 9. CHIN | = | $(NI_t - NI_{t-1})/NI_t + NI_{t+1})$, where $NI_t$ is Net Income for the most recent period. |

*Source*: Ohlson, J.A., *Journal of Accounting Research*, Spring, 1980.

## *APPENDIX G*

### Frederikslust's Estimated Chances of Misclassification

| Prediction Year | % Error Rates Initial Sample | | | % Error Rates Secondary Sample |
|---|---|---|---|---|
| | Non-failed Group | Failed Group | Average | Average |
| 1. | 05.0 | 10.0 | 07.5 | 08.0 |
| 2. | 15.0 | 20.0 | 17.5 | 15.0 |
| 3. | 25.0 | 20.0 | 22.5 | 22.0 |
| 4. | 25.0 | 30.0 | 27.5 | 30.0 |
| 5. | 25.0 | 35.0 | 30.0 | 33.0 |

*Source*: Frederikslust 1978, p. 52 and p. 110.

*APPENDIX H*

**Frederikslust's Estimated Chances of Misclassification**

| Year Before Failure | Percent Error Rates | | |
|---|---|---|---|
| | Non-failed Group | Failed Group | Average |
| 1. | 05.6 | 11.1 | 08.3 |
| 2. | 11.1 | 22.2 | 16.7 |
| 3. | 16.7 | 22.2 | 19.4 |
| 4. | 16.7 | 27.8 | 22.2 |

*Source:* Frederikslust, 1978, p. 67.

*APPENDIX I*

**Predictive Accuracy of Kaveri's Model**

| Year Before the Event | Initial Sample | Hold Out Sample |
|---|---|---|
| | Percent Correctly Classified | Percent Correctly Classified |
| 1. | 76.00 | 69.00 |
| 2. | 69.42 | 67.41 |
| 3. | 66.67 | 69.51 |
| 4. | 60.87 | 67.30 |
| 5. | 65.00 | 62.06 |
| 6. | 64.70 | 52.63 |
| 7. | 57.14 | 53.84 |

*Source*: Kaveri, V.S., 'Financial Ratios as Predictors of Borrower's Health', p. 218.

## *APPENDIX J*

### Srivastava's Percentage Error Rates in Classifying Between the Sick and Healthy Units

| S. No. | Ratios used in Discriminant Function | Misclassification Error |
|---|---|---|
| 1. | First Three Financial Ratios | 15% |
| 2. | Five Financial Ratios | 10% |
| 3. | First three Financial Ratios and one operational and one technical ratio | 5% |
| 4. | Five Financial Ratios, one operational and one technical ratio. | Nil |

*Source*: Srivastava, S.S., [56 p. 18].

## *APPENDIX K*

### List of Companies in the Initial Sample: Failed Companies

| *Co. Code No.* | *Name of the Company* |
|---|---|
| 101 | Cawnpore Industries Ltd. |
| 102 | Glucose and Food Ltd. |
| 103 | Mysore Chemicals and Fertilisers Ltd. |
| 104 | Eastern Woolen Mills Ltd. |
| 105 | South Bihar Sugar Mills Ltd. |
| 106 | Krishna Silicate Glass Works Ltd. |
| 107 | Radha Gobind Industries Ltd. |
| 108 | Tech. Glass Ltd. |
| 109 | Atlas Iron and Alloys Ltd. |
| 110 | The Sagar Mal Spinning and Weaving Mills Ltd. |
| 111 | Vidharbha Fertilisers and Chemicals Ltd. |
| 112 | The Ganges Printing and Ink Factory Ltd. |
| 113 | The Thakurdas Surekha Foundry Ltd. |
| 114 | The Dholpur Glass Works Ltd. |
| 115 | The Mysore Electro Chemicals Ltd. |
| 116 | The Moharani Parvati Sugar Mills Ltd. |
| 117 | Trianthrene Dyes, Drugs and Organics Ltd. |
| 118 | The Alexendra Jute Mills Ltd. |
| 119 | The Prabhuram Mills Ltd. Kottayam |
| 120 | Chamudhi Chemicals and Fertilisers Ltd. |
| 121 | M/s Micro Tools Ltd. |
| 122 | The Dacca Auyervedic Pharmacy Ltd. |
| 123 | Sree Yallana Cotton, Woollen and Silk Mills Ltd. |
| 124 | The Bhavnagar Vegetable Products Ltd. |
| 125 | Mohini Sugar Mills Ltd. |
| 126 | The Star Tiles Works Ltd. |
| 127 | Engel India Machines and Tools Ltd. |

| *Co. Code No.* | *Name of the Company* |
|---|---|
| 128 | Indian Paper and Pulp Company Ltd. |
| 129 | D.N. Chowdhry Cotton Mills Ltd. |
| 130 | Metal Press Works Ltd. |
| 131 | The National Screw and Wire Products Ltd. |
| 132 | Sidhpur Mills Company Ltd. |
| 133 | Keyjoy Spiroll Ltd. |
| 134 | Bihar Mica Syndicate Ltd. |
| 135 | National Pipes and Tubes Company Ltd. |
| 136 | U.P. Glass Works Ltd. |
| 137 | Union Paper and Board Mills Ltd. |
| 138 | Zenith Lamps and Electricals Ltd. |
| 139 | Britania Engineering Works Ltd. |

**Non Failed Companies**

| | |
|---|---|
| 240 | Jayaram Mills Ltd. |
| 241 | Hyderabad Roller Flour Mills Co. Ltd. |
| 242 | Travencore Chemical and Mfg. Co. Ltd. |
| 243 | Sudharshan Textiles and Chemicals Ltd. |
| 244 | The Phaltan Sugar Works Ltd. |
| 245 | Ogale Glass Works Ltd. |
| 246 | The Hooghly Flour Mills Co. Ltd. |
| 247 | The Mysore Stone Ware Pipes and Potteries Ltd. |
| 248 | Ram Cast Ltd. |
| 249 | Shri Kamapiran Mills Ltd. |
| 250 | Little's Oriental Balm and Pharmaceutical Ltd. |
| 251 | Krishan Lal Thirani and Co. Ltd. |
| 252 | The Binani Metal Works Ltd. |
| 253 | The Ishwar Industries Ltd. |
| 254 | Mysore Electrical Industries Ltd. |
| 255 | The Ratna Sugar Mills Ltd. |
| 256 | Keytuo Chemicals Ltd. |

| *Co. Code No.* | *Name of the Company* |
|---|---|
| 257 | The Dalhousie Jute Co. Ltd. |
| 258 | Madras Spinners Ltd. |
| 259 | Borax Morarji Ltd. |
| 260 | Tata Robins Fraser Ltd. |
| 261 | Frank Ross and Co. Ltd. |
| 262 | The Bombay Silk Mills Ltd. |
| 263 | Food Specialities Ltd. |
| 264 | The Bhopal Sugar Industries Ltd. |
| 265 | Thomas Steephen and Co. Ltd. |
| 266 | Usha Telehoist Ltd. |
| 267 | Pudumjee Pulp and Paper Mills Ltd. |
| 268 | Shree Sajjan Mills Ltd. |
| 269 | Rashtriya Metal Industries Ltd. |
| 270 | Hind Wires Industries Ltd. |
| 271 | Rustam Mills and Industries Ltd. |
| 272 | Indabrator Ltd. |
| 273 | Neveli Ceramics and Refractories Ltd. |
| 274 | Graham Firth Steel Products Ltd. |
| 275 | The Travancore Ogale Glass Mfg. Co. Ltd. |
| 276 | The Melamine and Fibre Board Ltd. |
| 277 | The Bengal Electrical Lamp Works Ltd. |
| 278 | Becos Engineering Works Ltd. |

## *APPENDIX L*

## The Eigenvalues of each Factor and the Percentage of Total Variance in the Data Explained by each Factor

### Group-1

| Factor | Eigenvalues | Portion | Cum. Portion |
|---|---|---|---|
| 1. | 7.886161 | 0.219 | 0.219 |
| 2. | 5.112642 | 0.142 | 0.361 |
| 3. | 4.493338 | 0.125 | 0.486 |
| 4. | 3.149981 | 0.087 | 0.583 |
| 5. | 2.595950 | 0.072 | 0.645 |
| 6. | 1.782762 | 0.050 | 0.695 |
| 7. | 1.570883 | 0.044 | 0.739 |
| 8. | 1.448913 | 0.040 | 0.779 |
| 9. | 1,227240 | 0.034 | 0.813 |
| 10. | 1.048450 | 0.029 | 0.842 |
| 11. | 0.898951 | 0.025 | 0.867 |
| 12. | 0.890760 | 0.025 | 0.892 |
| 13. | 0.796188 | 0.022 | 0.914 |
| 14. | 0.671642 | 0.019 | 0.933 |
| 15. | 0.477862 | 0.013 | 0.946 |
| 16. | 0.443137 | 0.012 | 0.958 |
| 17. | 0.351480 | 0.010 | 0.968 |
| 18. | 0.275149 | 0.008 | 0.976 |
| 19. | 0.239446 | 0.007 | 0.982 |
| 20. | 0.174923 | 0.005 | 0.987 |
| 21. | 0.110038 | 0.003 | 0.990 |
| 22. | 0.093472 | 0.003 | 0.993 |
| 23. | 0.080576 | 0.002 | 0.995 |
| 24. | 0.056733 | 0.002 | 0.997 |
| 25. | 0.050457 | 0.001 | 0.998 |
| 26. | 0.025088 | 0.001 | 0.999 |

Appendix L (*Contd.*)

| Factor | Eigenvalues | Portion | Cum. Portion |
|---|---|---|---|
| 27. | 0.017241 | 0.001 | 0.999 |
| 28. | 0.011588 | 0.000 | 1.000 |
| 29. | 0.009331 | 0.000 | 1.000 |
| 30. | 0.004402 | 0.000 | 1.000 |
| 31. | 0.002879 | 0.000 | 1.000 |
| 32. | 0.001572 | 0.000 | 1.000 |
| 33. | 0.000493 | 0.000 | 1.000 |
| 34. | 0.000111 | 0.000 | 1.000 |
| 35. | 0.000051 | 0.000 | 1.000 |
| 36. | 0.000012 | 0.000 | 1.000 |
| | **Group-2** | | |
| 1 | 10.812709 | 0.300 | 0.300 |
| 2 | 6.064019 | 0.169 | 0.469 |
| 3 | 4.951319 | 0.138 | 0.607 |
| 4 | 2.713621 | 0.075 | 0.682 |
| 5 | 2.148450 | 0.060 | 0.742 |
| 6 | 1.824108 | 0.051 | 0.792 |
| 7 | 1.420823 | 0.039 | 0.832 |
| 8 | 1.044257 | 0.029 | 0.861 |
| 9 | 0.944277 | 0.026 | 0.887 |
| 10 | 0.840003 | 0.023 | 0.910 |
| 11 | 0.710091 | 0.020 | 0.930 |
| 12 | 0.657528 | 0.810 | 0.948 |
| 13 | 0.384217 | 0.011 | 0.959 |
| 14 | 0.321634 | 0.009 | 0.968 |
| 15 | 0.257863 | 0.007 | 0.975 |
| 16 | 0.216995 | 0.006 | 0.981 |
| 17 | 0.196139 | 0.005 | 0.987 |
| 18 | 0.123854 | 0.003 | 0.990 |
| 19 | 0.102984 | 0.003 | 0.993 |

Appendix L (*Contd.*)

| Factor | Eigenvalues | Portion | Cum. Portion |
|---|---|---|---|
| 20 | 0.062515 | 0.002 | 0.995 |
| 21 | 0.057317 | 0.001 | 0.996 |
| 22 | 0.039783 | 0.001 | 0.997 |
| 23 | 0.036406 | 0.001 | 0.998 |
| 24 | 0.020312 | 0.001 | 0.999 |
| 25 | 0.015147 | 0.001 | 1.000 |
| 26 | 0.009193 | 0.000 | 1.000 |
| 27 | 0.005534 | 0.000 | 1.000 |
| 28 | 0.004935 | 0.000 | 1.000 |
| 29 | 0.001773 | 0.000 | 1.000 |
| 30 | 0.000867 | 0.000 | 1.000 |
| 31 | 0.000780 | 0.000 | 1.000 |
| 32 | 0.000368 | 0.000 | 1.000 |
| 33 | 0.000131 | 0.000 | 1.000 |
| 34 | 0.000030 | 0.000 | 1.000 |
| 35 | 0.000016 | 0.000 | 1.000 |
| 36 | 0.000002 | 0.000 | 1.000 |

*APPENDIX M*

## List of Companies in the Additional Samples

### APPENDIX M-1: **List of Failed Companies: Non-Homogeneous**

| *Co. Code No.* | *Name of the Company* |
|---|---|
| F–01 | Rubby Rubber Works (Madras) Ltd. |
| F–02 | M/s T.C.C. Appliances (Hyderabad) Ltd. |
| F–03 | Nagpal Plastics (Bombay) Ltd. |
| F–04 | The Gril Ltd. Ahmedabad |
| F–05 | Spence Ltd. |
| F–06 | Grant James Ltd. |
| F–07 | Borewell Tools Ltd. |
| F–08 | Benalee Engineering Works Ltd. |
| F–09 | Gwalior and Malwa Industries Ltd. |
| F–10 | Beta Pickers Ltd. |
| F–11 | Swastic Machanists Ltd. |
| F–12 | The Beavar Wool Pressing Co. Ltd. |
| F–13 | The Rampur Timber and Turning Co. Ltd. |
| F–14 | Rubber and Plastics Ltd. Kottoyam |
| F–15 | Meters and Measurement Ltd. Madras |
| F–16 | Hoisting Equipment Company Ltd. |
| F–17 | Hindustan Ceramic and Tiles Works Ltd. |
| F–18 | The Nagargali Cement Co. Ltd. |
| F–19 | The Oriental Potteries Ltd. |
| F–20 | Alamckal Company Ltd. |
| F–21 | Anant Starch Products Ltd. |
| F–22 | Burn and Company Ltd. |
| F–23 | Jessop and Co. Ltd. |
| F–24 | Hindustan Polymers Ltd. |

## Appendix M-2: List of Sick Textile Companies

| *Co. Code No.* | *Name of the Company* |
|---|---|
| ST–01 | The Algappa Textiles Ltd. Cochin |
| ST–02 | The Retlad Bulakhidas Mills Ltd. |
| ST–03 | The Cauvery Spg. and Wvg. Mills Ltd. |
| ST–04 | The Cannanore Spg. and Wvg. Mills Ltd. |
| ST–05 | The Appollo Mills Ltd. |
| ST–06 | The Ahmedabad New Textile Mills Ltd. |
| ST–07 | The Aurangabad Mills Ltd. |
| ST–08 | The Ahmedabad Jupiter Spg., Wvg. and Mfg. Co. Ltd. |
| ST–09 | The Arti Cotton Mills Ltd. |
| ST–10 | The Balram Verma Textiles Ltd. |
| ST–11 | The Coimbatore Spg. and Wvg. Co. Ltd. |
| ST–12 | The Mahboob Shahi Kulburga Mills Co. Ltd. |
| ST–13 | The Mysore Spg. and Mfg. Co. Ltd. |
| ST–14 | The New Maneck Chock Spg. and Wvg. Co. Ltd. |
| ST–15 | The Model Mills Nagpur Ltd. |
| ST–16 | The Mahalakshmi Ltd. Bhavnagar |
| ST–17 | The New Victoria Mills Co. Ltd. |
| ST–18 | The Minerva Mills Ltd. |
| ST–19 | The Osmanshahi Mills Ltd. |
| ST–20 | Sri Sarda Mills Ltd. |
| ST–21 | The Swadeshi Cotton and Flour Mills Ltd. |
| ST–22 | Tirputi Cotton Mills Ltd. |
| ST–23 | Vijay Mohini Mills Ltd. |
| ST–24 | Sri Rangvilas Ginning, Spg. and Wvg. Co. Ltd. |
| ST–25 | The Hira Mills Ltd. |
| ST–26 | The Himabai Mfg. Co. Ltd. |
| ST–27 | The Burhampur Tapti Mills Ltd. |
| ST–28 | The Azamjahi Mills Ltd. |
| ST–29 | The India United Mills Ltd. |

| *Co. Code No.* | *Name of the Company* |
|---|---|
| ST–30 | The Indore Malwa United Mills Ltd. |
| ST–31 | The Jehangir Vakil Mills Co. Ltd. |
| ST–32 | Elphenstone Spg. and Wvg. Mills Co. Ltd. |
| ST–33 | Finaly Mills Ltd. |
| ST–34 | The Gold Mohur Mills Ltd. |
| ST–35 | The Kohinoor Mills Co. Ltd. |
| ST–36 | Shri Madhusadan Mills Ltd. |
| ST–37 | The Tata Mills Ltd. |
| ST–38 | The Podar Mills Ltd. |

## APPENDIX M-3: **List of Non-Sick Textile Companies**

| | |
|---|---|
| NFT–01 | The New Swadeshi Mills of Ahmedabad Ltd. |
| NFT–02 | The Birla Cotton Spg. and Wvg. Mills Ltd. |
| NFT–03 | The Davangere Cotton Mills Ltd. |
| NFT–04 | Shri Vivekanand Mills Ltd. |
| NFT–05 | The Khatan Makanji Spg. and Wvg. Co. Ltd. |
| NFT–06 | Loyal Textiles Mills Ltd. |
| NFT–07 | Sri Krishna Rajendra Mills Ltd. |
| NFT–08 | Madura Coats Ltd. |
| NFT–09 | Maheshwari Mills Ltd. |
| NFT–10 | Matulya Mills Ltd. |
| NFT–11 | The Mahendra Mills Ltd. |
| NFT–12 | Piramal Spg. and Wvg. Mills Ltd. |
| NFT–13 | Svadeshi Mills Co. Ltd. |
| NFT–14 | The Khandesh Spg. and Wvg, Mills Co. Ltd. |
| NFT–15 | The Ahmedabad Kaiswer-i-Hind Mills Co. Ltd. |
| NFT–16 | The Ajit Mills Ltd. |
| NFT–17 | The Ahmedabad Shri Ram Krishna Mills Ltd. |
| NFT–18 | Mettur Beardsell Ltd. |
| NFT–19 | The Arvind Mills Ltd. |
| NFT–20 | Asoko Mills Ltd. |
| NFT–21 | The Bharat Survodaya Mills Co. Ltd. |

| *Co. Code No.* | *Name of the Company* |
|---|---|
| NFT–22 | Bowreah Cotton Mills Co. Ltd. |
| NFT–23 | The Hukam Chand Mills Ltd. |
| NFT–24 | The Dawn Mills Co. Ltd. Bombay |
| NFT–25 | The Dewan Bahadur Ramgopal Mills Ltd. |
| NFT–26 | Podar Projects Ltd. |
| NFT–27 | Rajapalayam Mills Ltd. |
| NFT–28 | Shiv Vallapa Textiles Ltd. |
| NFT–29 | Aditya Mills Ltd. |
| NFT–30 | Bilaspur Spg. Mills and Industries Ltd. |
| NFT–31 | Jawahar Mills Ltd. |
| NFT–32 | Rayalaseema Mills Ltd. |
| NFT–33 | Ajanta Textiles Ltd. |
| NFT–34 | Asher Textiles Ltd. |
| NFT–35 | The Nutan Mills Ltd. |

## Appendix M-4: **List of Non-Sick Jute Companies**

| | |
|---|---|
| NFJ–01 | Kamashathy Co. Ltd. |
| NFJ–02 | Cheviot Co. Ltd. |
| NFJ–03 | The General Industries Society Ltd. |
| NFJ–04 | Anglo-India Jute Mills Ltd. |
| NFJ–05 | Delta Jute Industries Ltd. |
| NFJ–06 | Nellimara Jute Mills Co. Ltd. |
| NFJ–07 | The Agarpara Co. Ltd. |
| NFJ–08 | Bally Jute Co. Ltd. |
| NFJ–02 | Birla Jute Manufacturing Co. Ltd. |
| NFJ–10 | The Champdany Jute Co. Ltd. |
| NFJ–11 | Fort Gloster Industries Ltd. |
| NFJ–12 | Hastings Mills Ltd. |
| NFJ–13 | Howrah Mills Co. Ltd. |
| NFJ–14 | Hukam Chand Jute Mills Ltd. |
| NFJ–15 | India Jute Co. Ltd. |

| *Co. Code No.* | *Name of the Company* |
|---|---|
| NFJ–16 | The Megna Mills Co. Ltd. |
| NFJ–17 | New Central Jute Mills Co. Ltd. |
| NFJ–18 | Reliance Jute and Industries Ltd. |
| NFJ–19 | The Nudda Company Ltd. |

## Appendix M-5: **List of Non-Sick Paper Companies**

| | |
|---|---|
| NFP–01 | The Western India Plywoods Ltd. |
| NFP–02 | Wood Polymer Ltd. |
| NFP–03 | Ballarpur Industries Ltd. |
| NFP–04 | Haryana Coated Papers Ltd. |
| NFP–05 | The Vidharbha Paper Mills Ltd. |
| NFP–06 | The West Coast Paper Mills Ltd. |
| NFP–07 | Ajay Paper Mills Ltd. |
| NFP–08 | Anil Hard Boards Ltd. |
| NFP–09 | Titaghur Paper Mills Co. Ltd. |
| NFP–10 | Venus Paper Mills Ltd. |
| NFP–11 | Seshasayee Paper and Boards Ltd. |
| NFP–12 | Star Paper Mills Ltd. |
| NFP–13 | Jayant Paper Mills Ltd. |
| NFP–14 | The National News Print and Paper Mills Ltd. |
| NFP–15 | The Andhra Pradesh Paper Mills Ltd. |
| NFP–16 | Sirpur Paper Mills Ltd. |
| NFP–17 | Utter Pardesh Straw and Agro Products |
| NFP–18 | Paper and Pulp Conversions Ltd. |
| NFP–19 | Balkrishna Paper Mills Ltd. |
| NFP–20 | Orient Paper Industries |
| NFP–21 | Perfect Pac Ltd. |
| NFP–22 | Rohit Pulp and Paper Mills Ltd. |
| NFP–23 | The Deccan Paper Mills Co. Ltd. |
| NFP–24 | Polymers Papers Ltd. |
| NFP–25 | Pondichery Papers Ltd. |
| NFP–26 | The Central Pulp Mills Ltd. |

| *Co. Code No.* | *Name of the Company* |
|---|---|
| NFP–27 | Pudumjeee Pulp and Paper Mills Ltd. |
| NFP–28 | The Malamine and Fibre Boards Ltd. |
| NFP–29 | The Western India Plywoods Ltd. |
| NFP–30 | Rolltainers Ltd. |

## APPENDIX M-6: **List of Non-Sick Chemical and Pharmaceutical Companies**

| | |
|---|---|
| NFCP–01 | Garware Plastics and Polymeters Ltd. |
| NFCP–02 | Chemicals and Plastics India Ltd. |
| NFCP–03 | Chemo Pharma Laboratories Ltd. |
| NFCP-04 | Cresent Dyes and Chemicals Ltd. |
| NFCP–05 | Herdellia Chemicals Ltd. |
| NFCP-06 | IDL Chemicals Ltd. |
| NFCP·07 | Lakme Ltd. |
| NFCP–08 | Mysore Petro Chemicals Ltd. |
| NFCP–09 | Nicholas Laboratories India Ltd. |
| NFCP–10 | Priyar Chemicals Ltd. |
| NFCP–11 | The Phosphate Co. Ltd. |
| NFCP–12 | Sudhana Nitro Chemicals Ltd. |
| NFCP–13 | Searsole Chemicals Ltd. |
| NFCP–14 | Terpene Industries Ltd. |
| NFCP–15 | Abbott Laboratories Ltd. (India) |
| NFCP–16 | Bharat Starch and Chemicals Ltd. |
| NFCP–17 | The Kutch Salt and Allied Industries Ltd. |
| NFCP–18 | Protein Products of India Ltd. |
| NFCP–19 | Adarsh Chemicals and Fertilisers Ltd. |
| NFCP–20 | Amines and Plasticizers Ltd. |
| NFCP–21 | BASF India Ltd. |

## APPENDIX M-7: **List of Non-Sick Iron and Steel Companies**

| | |
|---|---|
| NFIS–01 | Anil Steel and Industries Ltd. |
| NFIS–02 | B.D. Steel Castings Ltd. |

| *Co. Code No.* | *Name of the Company* |
|---|---|
| NFIS–03 | Bundy Tubings of India Ltd. |
| NFIS–04 | Canara Steel Ltd. |
| NFIS–05 | EL Forge Ltd. |
| NFIS–06 | Fit Tight Nuts and Bolts Ltd. |
| NFIS–07 | Galada Continuous Castings Ltd. |
| NFIS–08 | Kap Steel Ltd. |
| NFIS–09 | Mohan Steel Ltd. |
| NFIS–10 | Muzafarnagar Steels Ltd. |
| NFIS–11 | The National Rollings and Steel Ropes Ltd. |
| NFIS–12 | National Standard Duncan Ltd. |
| NFIS–13 | Punjab Concast Steels Ltd. |
| NFIS–14 | Rathi Alloys and Steel Ltd. |
| NFIS–15 | Ravindra Steel Ltd. |
| NFIS–16 | Roneo Vickers India Ltd. |
| NFIS–17 | Allied Steels Ltd. |
| NFIS–18 | Deepak Industries Ltd. |
| NFIS–19 | Durrung Steels Ltd. |
| NFIS–20 | Mohatta and Hecket Ltd. |

## Appendix M-8: **List of Non-Sick General Engineering (Machinery and Accessories) Companies**

| | |
|---|---|
| NFGE–01 | The ACME Manufacturing Ltd. |
| NFGE–02 | The Atlas Cycle Industries Ltd. |
| NFCE–03 | Engine Values Ltd. |
| NFGE–04 | Fuel Injections Ltd. |
| NFGE–05 | G-G Dandekar Machine Works Ltd. |
| NFGE–06 | Gujrat Automotive Gears Ltd. |
| NFGE-07 | International Instruments Ltd. |
| NFGE–08 | J.K. Business Machines Ltd. |
| NFGE–09 | Kerry Tost Tools Ltd. |
| NFGE–10 | Mopeds India Ltd. |
| NFGE–11 | Rexroth Maneklal Industries Ltd. |

| *Co. Code. No.* | *Name of the Company* |
|---|---|
| NFGE–12 | Sharma Engine Valve Ltd. |
| NFGE–13 | Shri Ram Pistons and Rings Ltd. |
| NFGE–14 | Tak Machinery Ltd. |
| NFGE–15 | Track Parts of India Ltd. |
| NFGE–16 | Anglo American Marine Co. Ltd. |
| NFGE–17 | Assotex Engineering Industries Ltd. |
| NFGE–18 | Beco Engineering Co. Ltd. |
| NFGE–19 | Indabrator Ltd. |
| NFGE–20 | I.A.E. (Bombay) Ltd. |
| NFGE–21 | International Combustion (India) Ltd. |

APPENDIX M-9: **List of Non-Sick Sugar Companies**

| | |
|---|---|
| NFS–01 | Arlem Breweries Ltd. |
| NFS–02 | Bharat Sugar Mills Ltd. |
| NFS–03 | Indo–Lwenbran Breweries Ltd. |
| NFS–04 | New India Sugar Mills Ltd. |
| NFS–05 | Ratna Sugar Mills Co. Ltd. |
| NFS–06 | Tulsipur Sugar Co. Ltd. |
| NFS–07 | The Ugar Sugar Works Ltd. |
| NFS–08 | The Vishnu Sugar Mills Ltd. |
| NFS–09 | Aruna Sugars Ltd. |
| NFS–10 | Belapur Sugar and Allied Industries Ltd. |
| NFS–11 | The Belsund Sugar Co. Ltd. |
| NFS–12 | The Bhopal Sugar Industries Ltd. |
| NFS–13 | Champasun Sugar Co. Ltd. |
| NFS–14 | The Gwalior Sugar Co. Ltd. |
| NFS–15 | Kothari Sugar and Chemicals Ltd. |
| NFS–16 | The New Swadeshi Sugar Mills Ltd. |
| NFS–17 | The Oudh Sugar Mills Ltd. |
| NFS–18 | Sakthi Sugars Ltd. |
| NFS–19 | South India Sugars Ltd. |
| NFS–20 | Upper Ganges Sugar Mills Ltd. |
| NFS–21 | The Maharashtra Sugar Mills Ltd. |

## Appendix M-10: **List of Non-Sick Electrical Companies**

| *Co. Code No.* | *Name of the Company* |
|---|---|
| NFE-01 | Bajaj Electricals Ltd. |
| NFE-02 | Bharat Bijlee Ltd. |
| NFE-03 | Eddy Current Controls (India) Ltd. |
| NFE-04 | Electrical Manufacturing Co. Ltd. |
| NFE-05 | Electro-Equipment Corporation Ltd. |
| NFE-06 | Emco Transformers Ltd. |
| NFE-07 | Gangappa Cables Ltd. |
| NFE-08 | Geep Industrial Syndicate Ltd. |
| NFE-09 | Air Control and Chemical Engineering Co. Ltd. |
| NFE-10 | General Electrodes and Equipment Ltd. |
| NFE-11 | International Computers Indian Manufacturing Ltd. |
| NFE-12 | Jay Electric Wire Corporation Ltd. |
| NFE-13 | Kaycee Industries Ltd. |
| NFE-14 | Kirloskar Systems Ltd. |
| NFE-15 | The Mysore Lamp Works Ltd. |
| NFE-16 | Punjab Anand and Batteries Ltd. |
| NFE-17 | Shri Ram Refrigeration Industries Ltd. |
| NFE-18 | Simco Meters Ltd. |
| NFE-19 | Willard India Ltd. |
| NFE-20 | Universals Ltd. |

## Appendix M-11: **List of Non-Sick Rubber Companies**

| | |
|---|---|
| NFR-01 | The Merrcarra Rubbers Ltd. |
| NFR-02 | The Rajagin Rubber and Produce Co. Ltd. |
| NFR-03 | Kailash Rubber Co. Ltd. |
| NFR-04 | Teekoy Rubbers (India) Ltd. |
| NFR-05 | The Velimalai Rubber Co. Ltd. |
| NFR-06 | The Pullangode Rubber and Produce Co. Ltd. |
| NFR-07 | The Malankara Rubber and Produce Co. Ltd. |
| NFR-08 | The Varkundam Rubber Co. Ltd. |
| NFR-09 | The Thirumbadi Rubber Co. Ltd. |
| NFR-10 | The Thamarapally Rubber Co. Ltd. |

# References

1. *Reserve Bank of India Report on Currency and Finance* 1978-79 to 1983-84.
2. Walter, J.E., *Determination of Technical Solvency* Journal of Business, 31, January 1957, pp. 30 43.
3. Donaldson, G., '*New Framework for Corporate Debt Policy*', Harvard Business Review, Vol. 40, March-April, 1962, pp. 117-31.
4. Donaldson, G., '*Strategy for Financial Emergencies*', Harvard Business Review, Nov-Dec. 1969, pp. 67-69.
5. Altman, E.I., *Corporate Bankruptcy in America* Lexington, Mass, D.C. Heath and Co., 1971, pp. 2-4.
6. Reserve Bank of India Report on '*Trend and Progress of Banking in India*' 1977-78, p. 25.
7. Chairman's Speech on 33rd Annual General Meeting of Industrial Finance Corporation of India (IFCI) Bombay.
8. Baruch Lev, *Financial Statement Analysis: A New Approach*', Prentice Hall, Inc., New Jersey, 1974, p. 134.
9. Laurant, L.R , *Improving the Efficiency and Effectiveness of Financial Ratio Analysis* Journal of Business Finance and Accounting, 1979, p. 401.
10. Beaver, W.H., Kennelly, J.W. and Voss, V.M., '*Predictive Ability as a Criterion for the Evaluation of Accounting Data*', The Accounting Review, 43 (October, 1968).
11. Ross, J.E. and Kami, M.J., '*Corporate Management in Crisis*', Prentice Hall, 1973.
12. Smith, R.A., *Corporations in Crisis,* Double Day, 1966.
13. Barmash, Isadore, '*Great Business Disaster*', Ballantine Books, 1973.
14. Robertson, Andrew, *The Lessons of Failure*, Macdonald, 1973.
15. John Argenti, *Corporate Collapse: The Causes and Symptoms*, McGraw-Hill, London, 1976.

16. John Argenti, '*The Anatomy of Company Failures: The Classical Syndrome*, The Accountant, May 6, 1976.
17. John Argenti, *Symptoms of Sickness*, Accounting, 1977, pp. 46-54.
18. A.F.L. Deeson, '*Great Company Crashes*, W. Foulsham and Co., London, 1972.
19. P.J. Fitz Patrick, '*A Comparison of Ratios of Successful Industrial Enterprises with those of Failed Firms*, Certified Public Accountant, 12 (October, November and December, 1932).
20. A. Winakor and R.F. Smith, '*Changes in Financial Structure of Unsuccessful Industrial Companies*', Bureau of Business Research Bulletin, No. 51, University of Illinois Press, 1935.
21. J.R. Ramser and L.O. Foster, '*A Demonstration of Ratio Analysis*', Bulletin No. 4 (Urbana: University of Illinois, Bureau of Business Research, 1931).
22. Merwin, C.L., '*Financing Small Corporations in Five Manufacturing Industries 1926-36*', New York: National Bureau of Economic Research, 1942.
23. W. Braddock Hickman, '*Corporate Bond Quality* and *Investors Experience*', Princeton University Press, 1958, pp. 390-421.
24. R.J. Saulinier; H.G. Halcrow and N.H. Jacoby, '*Federal Lending and Loan Insurance*', Princeton University Press, 1958, pp. 456-81.
25. G.H. Moore and Atkinson, '*Risk and Returns in Small Business Financing Towards a Firmer Basis of Economic Policy*', 41st Annual Report National Bureau of Economic Research, 1961, pp. 66-67.
26. M.H. Seiden, '*Trade Credit: A Quantitative and Qualitative Analysis Tested Knowledge of Business Cycles*, 42nd Annual Report National Bureau of Economic Research, 1962, pp. 86-88.
27. Beaver, W.H., '*Financial Ratios as Predictors of Failure*', Empirical Research in Accounting: Selected Studies, 1966, Supplement to Vol. 4, Journal of Accounting Research, pp. 71-127.
28. Beaver, W.H., '*Alternative Accounting Measures as Predic-*

*tors of Failure*', Accounting Review, Volume 43, January 1968, pp. 113-222.

29. Beaver, W.H., '*Market Prices, Financial Ratios and the Prediction of Failure*', Journal of Accounting Research, 6 (Autumn, 1968), pp. 179-192.
30. M. Tamari, '*Financial Ratios as a measure of Forecasting Bankruptcy*', Management International Review, Vol. 4, 1966, pp. 15-21.
31. Altman, E.I., '*Financial Ratios, Discriminant Analysis and the Prediction of Corporate Bankruptcy*', Journal of Finance, Vol. XXIII, September 1968, pp. 589-609.
32. Altman, E.I., Haldeman, Robert, G. and Narayanan, P., '*Zeta Analysis: A New Model to Identify Bankruptcy Risk of Corporations*', Journal of Banking and Finance, Spring, 1977.
33. Altman, E.I. and T.P. McGough, *Evaluation of a Company as a Going Concern*', Journal of Accounting, December 1974, pp. 50-57.
34. Altman, E.I. and Arnold. W. Sametz, '*Financial Crisis: Institutions and Markets in a Fragile Environment*', John Wiley and Sons, New York, 1977.
35. Altman, E.I., '*Corporate Bankruptcy Prediction and Its Implications for Commercial Loan Evaluations*', The Journal of Commercial Bank Lending, December 1970, pp. 8-12.
36. Altman, E.I., '*A Reply to Graig Johnson's Ratio Analysis and the Prediction of Firm Failure*', Journal of Finance, December 1970, pp. 1169-72.
37. Edward, B. Deakin, '*A Discriminant Analysis of Predictors of Failure*', Journal of Accounting Research, Vol. 1, No. 10, Spring, 1972, pp. 167-179.
38. Meyer, P.A. and Pifer, H.W., '*Prediction of Bank Failures*', Journal of Finance', Vol. XXV Sept., 1970, pp. 853-68.
39. Marc Blum, '*Failing Company Discriminant Analysis*', Journal of Accounting Research, Spring 1974, pp. 1-25.
40. Richard Taffler and Howard Tisshaw, '*Going, Going, Gone—Four Factors which Predict Failure*', Accountancy, March, 1977, pp. 50-54.
41. Ohlson, James A., '*Financial Ratios and the Probabilistic Prediction of Bankruptcy*', Journal of Accounting Research, Spring 1980, pp. 109-131.

42. Damolena, Ismael G. and Sarkis J. Khoury, '*Ratio Stability and Corporate Failure*', Journal of Finance, September 1980, pp. 1026-1071.
43. R.A.I. Van Frederikslust, '*Predictability of Corporate Failure*', Martinus Nyhoff Social Science Division Leiden/ Boston, 1978.
44. Luchenbruch, P.A., '*An Almost Unbiased Method of Obtaining Confidence Intervals for the Probability of Misclassification in Discriminant Analysis*', Biometrics, December 1969, pp 639-45.
45. Luchenbruch, P.A. and Micky, M.R., '*Estimation of Error Rates in Discriminant Analysis*', Technometrics, Vol. 10, No. 11.
46. J.W. Wilcox, '*Gambler's Ruin Approach to Business*', Sloan Management Review, Vol. 18, 1976, pp. 33-46.
47. Baruch Lev, '*Financial Failures and Informational Decomposition Measures, Accounting in Perspective: Contributions to Accounting Thought by other Disciplines,* R.R. Sterling and W.F. Bentz, South Western Publishing Co. 1971, pp. 102-111.
48. Elam, Rick, '*The Effect of Lease Data on the Predictive Ability of Financial Ratios*', Accounting Review, January 1975, pp. 25-43.
49. Aharony, Joseph; Charles, P. Jones and Itzhak, Swary, '*An Analysis of Risk and Return Characteristics of Corporate Bankruptcy using Market Data*', Journal of Finance, September, 1980, pp. 1001-1017.
50. Walker, M.C.; J.D. Stowe and S. Moriarty, '*Decomposition Analysis of Financial Statements*', Journal of Business and Accounting, Summer 1979, pp. 173-186.
51. John Argenti, '*Company Failure—Long-Range Prediction not Enough*', Accountancy, August 1977, pp. 40-48, 50, 52.
52. Gupta, L.C., '*Financial Ratios as Forewarning Indicators of Corporate Sickness*', A Study Sponsored by the Industrial Credit and Investment Corporation of India Ltd., Bombay, 1979.
53. Gupta, L.C., '*Financial Ratios for Monitoring Corporate Sickness*', Oxford University Press, 1983.
54. Gupta, L.C., '*Detecting Industrial Sickness*', Update, January 25-31, 1984, pp. 20-22.

55. Kaveri, V.S., '*Financial Ratios as Predictors of Borrower's Health*', Sultan Chand and Sons, New Delhi, 1980.
56. Srivastava, S.S., '*Design and Development of Information Systems for Development Banks: A System Approach*', Second IFCI Lecture, Faculty of Management Studies, University of Delhi, Feb. 1981, pp. 11-27.
57. Sarama, L.V.L.N. and Rao, G.B., '*Financial Ratios as Predictors of Failure: A Multivariate Approach*', Indian Manager, Vol. 7, (April-June 1976), pp. 175-189.
58. Pande, K.M. and Bhattacharya, C.D., '*Corporate Financial Strength: Application of Discriminant Analysis*', Jodhpur Management Journal (Published by Faculty of Commerce, University of Jodhpur), Vol. 3, pp. 23-26.
59. Chatterjee, S. and Roy, S., '*Forecasting Sickness: A Quantitative Approach*', 20th All India Cost Conference, Calcutta, January, 1978.
60. Vinod Kumar, '*Predictive Capability and Usefulness of Financial Ratios*', Unpublished Ph.D. Thesis.
61. Samuels, J.M. and Smyth, D.J., '*Profit, Variability of Profits and Firm Size*', Econometrica, 1968, pp. 127-139.
62. Horrigan, J.O., '*Some Empirical Bases of Financial Ratio Analysis*', Accounting Review, July 1965, Vol. 40, pp. 558-568.
63. Horrigan, J.O., '*The Determination of Long-term Credit Standing with Financial Ratios*', Empirical Research in Accounting: Selected Studies, 1966, Supplement to Vol. 4, Journal of Accounting Research, pp. 44-62.
64. Ball, R. and Brown, P., '*Some Preliminary Findings on the Association between the Earnings of the Firm, its Industry and the Economy*', Empirical Research in Accounting: Selected Studies, 1967, Supplement to Journal of Accounting Research, 1967, pp. 55-77.
65. James, H. Bliss, '*Financial and Operating Ratios in Management*', New York: The Ronald Press Co., 1923, p. 59.
66. A.C. Littleton, '*The 2 to 1 Ratio Analyzed*', Certified Public Accountant, August 1926, pp. 244-46.
67. Sidney, Alexander, '*The Effect of Size of Manufacturing Corporation on the Distribution of the Rate of Return*',

Review of Economics and Statistics, August 1919, pp. 229-235.

68. Gilman, Stephen, '*Analyzing Financial Statements*', The Ronald Fress Company, New York, 1925.
69. Guthmann, Harry, '*Analysis of Financial Statements*', Prentice Hall, Inc., New York.
70. Foulke, Roy A., '*Practical Financial Statement Analysis*', 6th Ed., McGraw-Hill Book Company, 1968.
71. Spencer, A. Tucker, '*Successful Managerial Control by Ratio Analysis*', McGraw-Hill Book Company, Inc. New York, 1961.
72. Irving, Kellogg, '*How to use Financial Statements*', McGraw-Hill Book Company, New York, 1969.
73. Myer, John M., '*Financial Statement Analysis*', Prentice Hall, Fourth Ed., 1969.
74. Eric, A. Helfert, '*Techniques of Financial Analysis*', Richard D. Irwin Inc., 1972.
75. Kennedy, R.D. and Mcmullen, S.Y., '*Financial Statements Forms, Analysis and Interpretation*', Homewood, Illinois, Richard D. Irwin Inc., 1973.
76. Bernstein, L.A., '*Financial Statement Analysis: Theory, Application and Interpretation*', Homewood, Illinois, Irwin, 1974.
77. Slater, S.D., '*The Strategy of Cash: A Liquidity Approach to Maximising the Company's Profit*', London, Wiley, 1974, pp. 287-368.
78. Tennent, M., '*Practical Liquidity Management*', Epping Gower Press, 1976, pp. 37-44, 175-179.
79. Foster, George, '*Financial Statement Analysis*', Prentice-Hall, Inc., New Jersey, 1978.
80. Theil, '*Principles of Econometrics*', John Wiley and Sons, New York, 1971, pp. 147-154.
81. Chudson, W.A., '*The Pattern of Corporate Financial Structure: A Cross-section View of Manufacturing, Mining, Trade and Construction Corporations*', 1937, New York: National Bureau of Economic Research, 1945.
82. Wozinlower, A.M., '*The Quality of Bank Loans: A Study of Bank Examination Records*', Occasional Paper No. 82 (New York: National Bureau of Economic Research, 1962, pp. 3-4).

83. Baruch Lev, '*Industry Averages as Targets for Financial Ratios*' Journal of Accounting Research, 7 (Autumn 1969), pp. 290-99.
84. Harry, H. Harman, '*Modern Factor Analysis*', The University of Chicago Press, 1977.
85. Hofstede, G.H., '*The Game of Budget Control*', (Van Gorcum 1967), p. 313.
86. Rummel, R.J., '*Applied Factor Analysis*', Evanston, Northwestern University Press, 1970, p. 379.
87. B. Fruchter, '*Introduction to Factor Analysis*', D. Van Nostrand Company, Inc., pp. 44-50.
88. Overall John E. and Klett, James, C., '*Applied Multivariate Analysis*', McGraw-Hill, 1972, pp. 243-279.
89. Fisher, R.A., '*The use of Multiple Measurements in Taxonomic Problems*', Annals of Eugencies No. 7, September 1936, pp. 179-188.
90. Cochran, W.G., '*On the Performance of the Linear Discriminant Function*', Technometrics, Vol. 6, May 1964, pp. 179-190.
91. Travers, R.M.W., '*The use of Discriminant Function in the Treatment of Psychological Group Differences*', Psychometrica, Vol. 4 No. 1, March, 1939, pp. 25-32.
92. Henry, E. Garret, '*The Discriminant Function and its use in Psychology*', Psychometrica, Vol. 8 No. 2, June 1943, pp. 65-79.
93. Durand, D.D., '*Risk Elements in Consumer Instalment Financing: Studies in Consumer Instalment Financing*', New York: National Bureau of Economic Research, 1941, pp. 105-142.
94. Myers, H. and Forgy, E.W., '*Development of Numerical Credit Evaluation Systems*', Journal of American Statistical Association, Vol. 50, September, 1963, pp. 797-806.
95. Walter, J.E., '*A Discrimination Function for Earnings Price Ratios of Large Industrial Corporation*', Review of Economics and Statistics, Vol. XLI (February, 1959), pp. 44-52.
96. Smith, K.V., '*Classification of Investment Securities using MDA*', Institute Paper 101 (Purdue Univ. Institute for Research in the Behavioral, Economic and Management Sciences, 1965).
97. Roenfeldt. Rohney L. and Cooley, Philip L., '*Predicting*

*Corporate Profitability for Investment Selection*', Journal of Business Finance and Accounting, Spring, 1978, pp. 57-65.

98. Bird, R.G. and McHugh, '*Financial Ratios: An Empirical Study*', Journal of Business Finance and Accounting, Spring 1977, pp. 29-45.
99. Deakin, E.B., '*Distributions of Financial Accounting Ratios: Some Empirical Evidence*', The Accounting Review, 1976, pp. 90-96.
100. Guthman and Dougall, '*Corporate Financial Policy*', Prentice Hall of India Ltd., New Delhi, 1969, p, 65.
101. Sidney Davidson; G.H. Sorter and Hemer Kalle, '*Measuring the Defensive Position of a Firm*', Financial Analysts Journal, 20 (January-February, 1964), pp. 23-29.
102. George, H. Sorter and George Benston, '*Appraising the Defensive Position of a Firm: The Internal Measure*', Accounting Review (October, 1960), pp. 633-40.
103. Donald D. Morrision, '*On the Interpretation of Discriminant Analysis*', Journal of Marketing Research, 6 (Ma 1969), p. 156.

# Index